SKIDDING IN SIDEWAYS

SKIDDING IN SIDEWAYS

A Southern Gentleman's Tale

Douglas McBride

iUniverse LLC
Bloomington

SKIDDING IN SIDEWAYS
A Southern Gentleman's Tale

iUniverse books may be ordered through booksellers or by contacting:

iUniverse LLC
1663 Liberty Drive
Bloomington, IN 47403
www.iuniverse.com
1-800-Authors (1-800-288-4677)

ISBN: 978-1-4917-2847-5 (sc)
ISBN: 978-1-4917-2846-8 (e)

Library of Congress Control Number: 2014905309

Printed in the United States of America.

iUniverse rev. date: 03/15/2014

What's In The Book

Hey Y'all!

I have had the notion to sit down and write a book for years. What I didn't have was the time or any semblance of a solid notion of how to put things to paper. The mess that follows here started life really as more a journal to pass on to my offspring and to theirs, long after I had left this world. Somewhere along the line, some friends of mine said, "Doc, you need to take this to the next level and maybe publish it." I'm thinking *Yah, bullshit, who's gonna read this?* However, I kept at it until I finally convinced myself to give publishing a shot and so here we are, on the verge of God knows what.

On any given day depending on what uniform I'm wearing, I am Doctor to my patients, Sir to the Army, Officer to those I arrest, Dad to my kids, baby to my wife and asshole to the guy I just flipped off for cutting me off in traffic. The reality is I'm a Southern redneck, country by the grace of God and the ordinary man you see every day as you go about your business—the one you never look twice at in Walmart or notice as I walk by. I am not famous, nor chummy with someone who is. I am not a millionaire and I'm not on any of those damn reality shows (I hate that shit). This book is about just a regular guy that makes up the backbone of our society and the majority of this country's workforce and population at large.

Let me start by telling you this: seeing as how I'm from the South, this is pretty much written the way I speak and think. I cuss a lot and sometimes in Technicolor but I don't apologize for this because it's my book and I'll speak the way I want. Anyhow, it gives it character and we down here are all about characters. If I offend you, oh well, get your money back. I don't have a dog in that fight and none of this is directed at you personally. I also want to point out to you folks north of the

Mason-Dixon line that just 'cause I talk slow doesn't mean I am. We do have indoor shitters, shoes on our feet and my sister isn't my mom, but of course, I can't speak for everyone on that one. In the South there are three things that are sacred and untouchable: church, family and football. No matter where you go in these parts, anyone and everyone will be an expert on any and all of them, especially football. Hell, for some of us football is church.

We have the stigma down here that Yankees seem to use as a measuring stick for us Southern folk. We talk a little different, eat things y'all think belong in a hog pen, and some of our words aren't the same, like reckon, gitcha, kinda, y'all, and fixin' to, but we are 100 % Americans, through and through. If you've never eaten road kill raccoon, gator, frog, possum or squirrel, you don't have a whole lot to say on this subject, now do ya. It's some good eating, so don't knock it till you've tried it. Y'all might wanna check your history, too, cause a good number of things came from the South that everyone benefits from today, starting with moonshine, NASCAR, air conditioning, Charlie Daniels, Duck Dynasty, Swamp people and the Road Kill Cookbook, just to name a few. If y'all are down here visiting, don't get liquored up and start talking about how y'all whipped our ass in the Civil War either, because someone is gonna get pissed and be on your ass like a tick on a hound. I guess some are still kinda touchy about that.

Oh yeah, I meant to tell y'all that for the most part I will be leaving people's real names and places out of this unless we have already agreed it's okay. If you figure or think I'm talking about you and don't like what I've said, well, what can I say. I hate it for you. My give-a-shit meter is way low on that one.

At first I thought I would get all philosophical and derive some magical meaning out of my life and share that with who ever gave a shit. Nope, boring and I still have no idea what that "magical meaning" might be, so scrap that idea. What about the lessons I have learned and how I got to where I am today? Hmmm . . . nah . . . . who would spend hours out of their lives to read about who and/or what has kicked my ass this far into the life cycle? The truth is, that I don't know the first damn thing about writing a book; hell, I can't even spell. Without the genius of computer spell and grammar check y'all would have no idea what I'm saying. I'm not functionally illiterate or anything; I just didn't pay enough attention in kindergarten through grade twelve English.

I felt like there were things that had occurred to me, happened to me, taught me and changed me enough to make me the asshole I am today. If I could get those down on paper it might be funny to some, retarded to others or maybe, just maybe, give others a lick of hope, some direction or a good laugh. Mostly I wanted my kids to have something to look at long after I have parted the ways and in some small way, still have a little of my guidance. I don't know why I would think like that; they don't listen to me now, so what makes me think that would change if I was dead?

I have not wasted my given time here under the sun and moon. I have been called the original "been there, done that" man by some. I have always set out to accomplish the next thing in a long line of stuff that goes back to when I was still shitting in my britches. I never was satisfied with normal. Had to do things faster, better, stronger, straighter, longer, bigger, brighter . . . . well, you get the idea. Why, I have no frigging idea; it was just in me to do it. Was I always the best or even in the top ten? Hell no, rarely even close but I got it done, then it was on to the next challenge life presented me with. My wife says I'm compulsive and obsessive when I get into something and she may be right. I'm just not going to admit she is right; that is unacceptable. No male in his right mind would do that.

What I am trying to say is I always wanted what was around the next bend in the road. I will admit at times my obsession with the next great idea was at the cost of time with those important to me. It's one of those things you don't see till you are looking at the ass end of it. As an example, training for Ironman races. I spent hours and hours on my bike, at the pool, and in the gym, all without my family. I would emerge every so often like the sloth from his cave, and eat, drink, burp, fart, sleep and take them with me while I raced. But other than that, there was about a three-year period there where I was held hostage to an obsession and pretty much left my family to their own devices. Not good any way you look at it, but having now confessed my guilt I don't know that there was another way to get it done.

If you look up the definition of triple "A" personality you will see what I look like. Try not to laugh; I was blessed in other ways. I never wanted to be just ordinary. My mom would tell me, "Don't try to live above your raising" and I didn't. I have always kept in mind where and what I came from. However, I did strive to know and be all that was needed by my family, friends and the people who relied on me. It was always if I didn't know, I was damn well gonna find out. This book is the same shit—never done it before so let's give it a whirl and figure it out as we go along. It will probably end up as toilet reading or ass-wipe, but so be it; it's done and nothing wasted but my time. Here I am two pages into just the introduction and I really haven't told y'all where this is going, have I? Well . . . that's because I don't know. I'm just sort of winging it till something jumps out at me as a good direction.

The humor of getting up and visiting the world every day is very amusing to me. As Gump's mama says, "It's a box of chocolates." Some days were unforgettable, whereas others needed poking in the eye with a sharp stick. Nonetheless, we have to go through them. There is no way to avoid the unpleasant life events like we would stepping over dog shit just in time. I prided myself for the most part being able to take what was handed to me and run with it. I didn't always run with grace but I got it done. At times I think I even managed to pick what I wanted from the chocolate box. I did not always make the right decision or choose the path of least resistance. I explored, experimented, poked prodded, pulled, pushed, clawed and bullshitted my way for the most part. Winston Churchill said, "That, my lovelies, is life, so get on with it." If you ever want some fine reading pick up his biography; it's awesome.

Reading is one of my great passions in life. I have always turned to books for answers and entertainment. My wife's long-standing attempt at humor is that when I don't know how to do something she tells me, "Go read a book" because she thinks it's funny that I actually do that. She and my kids get great delight in calling me egghead. I have learned how to do more shit from getting the book on it than I ever did in a classroom. I hated sitting in class and even in Medical school it sucked. I went to the classes I needed to and skipped the rest and probably attended only about two-thirds of the classes. I wasn't out partying or fucking off somewhere. I got the work done but did it my way. Now I'm not saying I didn't party and do some fucking off; that would be a bold face lie 'cause party we did, but not at the cost of school, just brain cells. I also won't tell you that I never walked into an exam hung over. Couldn't have been that bad; I graduated fifth out of two hundred. My point: if I want to learn how to do something, I buy a book and guess what, there isn't a book on how to write a book like this. At least one that has my outstanding grasp of grammar and vocabulary.

Apparently I was born with an above-average IQ according to the testing that was done, and I have one of those strange memories that goes along with it. It sort of takes pictures and little home movies. This would be nice and convenient if you got to choose what you played back and kept, but mine doesn't work that way. My momma will be quick to tell you, "You'd think as smart as that boy is, he would have the sense to walk around right and get across the street on his own, but he don't.". The fact is, smart don't come with sense. In university, one of the ways I made a little extra cash was as a lab rat for the psychology department. They didn't stick me or probe me in places only ET would go, but they would give me test after test to do under different conditions. For example, dexterity tests without sleep, loud music playing or drunk and so on. What they found was I was not as retarded as everyone thought and I had this funky memory thing with a learning disability. Whoa! What? I'm LD? According to these guys, even though I have the memory thing and IQ thing, I can still have an LD thing. The examples they gave me were Da Vinci and Einstein. Apparently these two had issues also. Two of the greatest minds in history were 'tards just like me. I could read and comprehend just fine; my malfunction was in dimensional mathematics. That fit too, because school was easy to me. Never really applied myself like I should because I didn't give a shit, but there was never anything as hard as math. The more I had to do, the dumber I got. Come to find out I really didn't hate it, I think I was just frustrated with it. (I'm pretty sure I hated it also.)

I had to take math in university and I was freaking out because not doing well could've prevented me from getting into Medical school. I had a friend, Rick, who was in engineering and great at math. I had Rick tutor me and this is how I got a whiff there was a problem before I even knew there really was one. When I tried to follow the steps in the book to solve the problem, I just wasn't catching on. When Rick showed me another way, BAM! It clicked and it was no problem with the rest of them. It was the way I did it, not what I was doing—what was later revealed to me as the "dimensions of mathematics." Apparently math is 3D; who knew? I never got the glasses they handed out in class, must have missed that day fucking off, I guess. Anyway it's a kind of thinking pattern that I don't have, so if you want to know more buy a book because that's where my understanding quits.

The memory thing is a whole other matter. Basically, if I do anything with my hands or see things in a pattern or continuously I will rarely forget it. I can remember shit I did as a kid like it was yesterday. The memories are not always complete at times because of the way it was presented to me, but I have about 90% recall. The psych boys called it "Partial recall". To me it's the home movie theater. There is really only one tiny problem . . . I have no choice to remember whatever it might be and that includes bad shit. A friend of mine in medical school had "total recall"—what we usually call a true photographic memory. Weird as hell, too, because he would read a textbook and then we would open it randomly tell him the page we were looking at, and he would recite verbatim what was on there. Needless to say, the bastard never failed any exams. My memory can't do that with words. I can't just look at a page and tell what was written, but if you put a picture with it I could tell you all day long. Weird, huh? I can still remember the face, name and circumstances of every child I've ever had to pronounce dead, like I said . . . everything, whether I want to or not. As a policeman this was an invaluable tool because I could remember details just by bringing the picture up in my head. I've had a couple of medical malpractice cases over the years that I had to give depositions for, and the opposing lawyer tried his best to un-screw my story even down to the smallest of details, but it never happened. If I didn't remember, it didn't happen.

As a side note, over the past 11 years my memory has failed me countless times—at least, that's what my wife says. According to her I don't remember shit, and she has to do all the remembering for us, especially when it comes to how our conversations really went. Amazing, ain't it? Sure glad she is around to keep me straight. Shit, before you know it, I'll have Alzheimer's disease, according to her.

Folks, it has been a ride like no other to this point in my tenure on this planet. I have had fun and heartbreak, easy lessons and some really hard ones. My dad told me over and over, from the time I was very small, "Life is not about arriving at the grave well preserved, pristine and unscarred. It's about Skidding in Sideways, full throttle, bent, dirty and tore up, screaming, 'Holy shit, what a ride!'" This is the mantra of my life and the way I live, folks, good or bad, right or wrong, and so without further ado, I would like to share some of the highlights with you. Just remember, I didn't make you read this, so I deny responsibility for any mental or visual issues you might endure.

BEING A KID

As a kid I don't remember the world being the shit hole it is today. I am the oldest of three, younger brother Steven followed by baby sister Kim. I thought being the oldest was a pain in the ass. I was the one always charged with "Keep an eye on your brother and sister", "You better not come home without them" "If you're going to the movies take them with you" and so on. Aw shit! Do I gotta?! 'Course I never said squat about it 'cause that would have cost me all of my front teeth; nonetheless, I still got pissed off having to drag them around with me. On any given day I'm in another zip code with my buddies at the fort or wherever and those two were wanting to come with me. It worked out most of the time. Usually it came down to me farming them out to whatever of their friends were around with the strict instructions they were not to go home without me. That way it looked like I had them with me the whole time.

It's odd, they were such a pain in the ass to me but if someone messed with them, it was on. You didn't mess with my brother and sister because that was a privilege reserved only for older brothers. They were the guinea pigs for all of my freshly-designed weapons of fort war and anything else I needed a human sacrifice for. It was a fair trade to me. I offered up protection from the world and they offered up life and limb in the name of science and weapons development. We had rules between us, as well: don't go in my room or touch my stuff and I won't come in the middle of the night and fuck you up. That was my brother's modus operandi; he would wait till I was asleep then hit me with something, usually a piece of furniture. He did it this way because I would beat his ass in any other scenario and I couldn't start a fight with him right then cause I would wake up our parents. I don't know if he thought I would forget about it and the next day act like nothing happened but that was never the case.

As kids Steve and I were probably the closest, especially into our teens. That went away over the years and as of this writing I have not seen or spoken to him in over 20 years. He did some shit to my mom that was not cool but instead of making it right he just cut us out of his life like we weren't even there. Thanks Steve, you asshole. And by the way Steve, if you ever read this, Mom is doing just fine—not that you'd care. My sister and I were the opposite in every way growing up and even today we can't agree on shit. I wouldn't say we are close but we are in each other's lives and Mom is our common thread. Sis is very smart and has done well in her family and career, and I am very proud of her. Tim, her husband, is ex-military and a little odd in my opinion, but he loves my sister and is a great dad so he's squared away in my book. Just don't ever ask him to do any carpentry work. I've seen his work and all I can say is damn, you might wanna go look on Angie's list is all I'm saying.

In the summer, my mom would boot our asses out the door post-breakfast and we were not seen again until lunch. That is, if we had lunch at our house. Most of the time we chowed at whichever kid's refrigerator was the closest 'cause we were busy with forts to build, frogs to catch, bikes to ride and neighborhoods to terrorize. Parents back then didn't worry because everyone watched out for the others' kids and property. We kids followed the shout rule, which meant you had to be in shouting distance of a grown up, and that was really about it. You would never even dream of letting that happen today. No siree bub, too many predators out there. Every day you hear about this child missing or this one found dead. You rarely see kids just out in the neighborhood playing on their own without a parent or parents hovering over them doing roll call every five minutes to make sure Freddie Kruger hadn't paid a visit. To be blunt and honest, I am afraid for my children and my grandchildren. This is not the place I thought I would be leaving them, and it's sad for a child to have to live that way. I treasure my childhood as probably the last of its kind.

There were rules to being a kid then and you followed them or took your licks. It was simple; you didn't speak around grownups if they were talking. You had a sir or ma'am on the end of every sentence. "No" was it, end of discussion. You got told/asked to do something once; after that it was your ass. You had chores that were done before anything else and the same went for homework, and you never even dreamed of raising your voice or sassing a grown up because that was a guaranteed ass whooping. When I was a kid an ass whooping was just that, an event that made it all crystal clear and unforgettable. School disputes were settled after school with your fists and then it was over. TV was an hour before bed, maybe, and that's if all your other shit was squared away. I could do this all day but I need to get on with the rest of this. The point I'm getting at is it's not like that anymore.

It's hot as hell in the South in the summer. I mean like two rats screwing in a wool sock kinda hot. Anyone who has been down here knows what I'm talking about. It really isn't the temperature so much as the humidity 'cause on any given day its 95 degrees with 98% humidity and it's like living in a fish tank. I loved being a kid because the summer was forever along with the greatest adventures I could dream up to make a reality. There was frog catching and gigging, and I mean not just a few either; we're talking by the bucket full. It was always a source of curiosity to me how the next day there were considerably fewer in the bucket than the day before. I think some got away with a little help from my mom but of course she would and did deny it. I have caught some big-ass bullfrogs none of which I'm pretty sure could lift a brick and a plank of wood off the top of a bucket—of course, that's just speculation on my part.

Gopher hunting with your Daisy BB gun was restricted to only those who had one and the best friend of the day allowed the privilege of coming with. Prowess was measured by actually being able to kill one, which is a very difficult thing to accomplish when you make a lot of noise, you smell, have no idea what you're doing and can't shoot for shit. Besides, trying to kill a gopher at 50 yards when the range on your daisy is only 25 at best just compounds the issue. None of this was a deterrent to us to go on safari every summer trying to catch squirrels, raccoons, birds and other assorted wildlife so we could try and talk our parents into letting us keep it, to make it "our pet". I spent hours and hours holding that string attached to the stick that held up the cardboard box waiting for some critter to go under it to eat the peanut butter on a piece of bread. Remember that shit? I never caught a dam thing except the neighbor's cat, and it took off with the box and the bread.

We always had a fort. It was always in a secret location entrusted to only the select few, and was the first order of business when gang members were being selected for the summer. (This was done based on some very biased and loose rules. Usually it involved personal hygiene and other things.) To recon a place to put the fort was a huge and detailed function. It involved the gang arguing for several hours, even days, to un-democratically but strategically agree on its placement. It had to be close to one of our houses in case of an emergency—you know, things like food and the call of nature. The ultimate site was in the air, more specifically, a tree. More than one trip to the hospital was the result of an unrestrained child worker on the fort falling out of said tree in the line of duty. The gang and by inclusion the fort had to have a bad-ass name on a flag or a sign. It just wasn't legit without it. I mean, did you ever read a war story where the armies in it were named "those guys"? No, you didn't, so agreeing on the name usually took the better part of the time it took to build the fort. An unspoken gang and fort rule was that there were no girls allowed. You were the complete asshole if you showed up with a girl at the fort. We really didn't give a fuck if it was your sister—no girls allowed. The reasoning was simple, based on the well-known fact girls could not keep their mouths shut and usually gave away all the secrets of the fort, including its location. They were considered a security risk.

The ultimate test for a gang and their fort was to be able to successfully defend it from an attack from a neighboring gang and to have a sleepover in it. War on another gang and their fort was inevitable and a rite of passage, really, especially for FNGs (fucking new guys). Slingshots, water bombs and elastic clothes pin guns were the weapons of choice. How we ever got to puberty with both eyes and all our limbs is a never-ending source of curiosity to me. The rules were simple: each side was given fair warning of a raid coming; when the losing fort was pillaged, said fort was given back to the losers minus what was pillaged, and no using big brothers to fight for ya. That was a serious breach in

11

fort etiquette that could get your ass kicked and banished from ever being a gang member again.

To and from transportation to the fort required you to have a minimum of six cards clothes-pinned to your front and back wheels, flipping past your spokes so you sounded bad ass driving your ride around the hood. Your bike was configured so you could double or triple as required. You were looked upon in awe by the others when you could triple ride, one on the front and one on the back. You were the BMOC then. The only bike skill that trumped this was being able to jump a drainage ditch with or without a take-off ramp and not wipe out. Our bikes were our prized possessions and a great source of pride as a kid. Hours were spent caring for and modifying them, only to be ditched at a moderate speed on the driveway at supper time, left in the rain or put through any manner of rigorous workdays. I could hitch a wagon to mine, and this proved to be very useful when it came to hauling fort materials, food and ammunition. The only real physics problem you had to be aware of was going down a hill applying your brakes, and the wagon laden with rocks and wood usually started to overtake the bike. Not an optimal scenario and very difficult to overcome without getting launched off the bike and getting very messed up.

When we weren't trying to kill one another or playing Evel Knievel with our bikes, there was often a multitude of other summer sports to choose from. Some were for pussies, like tennis or golf, which we had no part in. The only real sports were football and baseball—ask any kid—whereas sports like golf tended to be age dependent, also. You didn't see a whole lot of 6 year olds teeing off at the first hole. We tended to be more on baseball in the summer but football was never out of the question. It's strange, even today you couldn't pay me to watch a baseball game live or on the TV 'cause it just bores the living hell out of me, but put a glove or bat in my hand and I will play all day. You ever notice there are certain smells that just go with baseball? I don't mean like fresh dog shit baking in the sun, I mean nostalgic smells that even today will bring back memories and times that make you all warm and fuzzy. I'm getting sidetracked again.

Baseball always seemed like a job to me. I had to work at it to be any good. I was a pitcher and prided myself on throwing fast and straight. At least more than the other pitchers in the league, I thought. I got an award one year that backed that statement up. Big frigging deal; it wasn't the Major Leagues, even though we thought it was. I never missed a game unless we were away or I was being punished for other dumb-ass things I'd done. The kids in the neighborhood would have an almost daily game of 300. This is where one guy hit the ball however he wanted to the guys in the field. Depending on what kind of ball you caught—grounder, line drive or a pop fly—was how many points you got. The first one to 300 got to bat, and I won't tell you no one cheated because we did. I also won't tell you we didn't hip check the fucker next to you so you could get his catch because maybe we did.

My dad made it to a lot of my games and we spent a lot of time playing catch and working on my pitches. I would practice with him so much that my glove hand would swell up and hurt like hell, but I wouldn't quit for nothing. The same went for hockey and football; no matter how it hurt, I would not quit. This kind of stupidity has served me well for the most part, but in these more recent years, when God seems to be taking away more than he is giving, my body has paid for these younger indulgences. Now I feel all the old injuries that were nothing to me back then. My brother hated to play any kind of sport and any chance he had to get out of playing, he would be so gone. Consequently, he wasn't much help with practicing

Hockey was my winter passion and occupation. I loved playing hockey but being from the South, ice rinks were not just around every corner. We lived in Canada for several years, so this was not an issue 'cause they have ice rinks in just about every backyard because the place stays half frozen most of the time. There was something about the way you could glide on the ice that always felt so cool to me. Of course, in the learning phases of skating gliding on your ass or your face did not fill me with the same amore, and that happened a lot.

I played defense man position and this required you to be able to skate backward almost as fast as you could forward, hence the gliding on my face and ass. This in my opinion was the hardest position for several reasons, but mostly because you were usually the only guy between a player on the other team with the puck and your goalie. Your job was basically to get in his way and disrupt this attack any way you could. This sometimes required you to take a puck in the nuts and this, boys and girls, educated me quick, fast and in a hurry on the true value of wearing a jock. My dad was a defense man playing hockey and was pretty good too, so I spent hours with him on the ice teaching me how to do the job. I played in what was known as the Pee Wee league and every year they would pick and all-star team called the "Bananas" to play other teams in other towns. This team was the Holy Grail that we all strived to get on. They had cool shit like matching jerseys with their name on it and helmets that were painted half yellow and half black. Cool stuff, man, and you were the shit if you got on the team. The president didn't have this kind of recognition, believe me. Sometimes the team would even be flown in a Chinook helicopter to away games compliments of the military, so as you can imagine, to a kid, that was total bragging rights. Anyway, the last season I played Pee Wee I made the Bananas. Ahh . . . to be king for a day.

We used our minds, imaginations and our bodies to make our forts and in the summer not a minute was wasted. Unfortunately, it appears to be a lost art with young'uns these days. The fort was summer central and a place where you bitched, moaned and whined to anyone who would listen, made plans to do other stuff outside of the usual day—to-day, and told all the bullshit stories you could get away with. It was great—nothing else to do, with no responsibilities outside of the usual chores and no worries, bills or kids.

The coolest day of the week to me, I think, was Saturday. It was the day after Friday, therefore no school and there was always shit planned for this two-day break from the world of gym class, math and the English teacher that smelled like ass. The best part was hamburgers. Mom made them every Saturday without fail and we got to have potato chips with them and no veggies, liver or other shit that just wasn't decent to a kid's palate. In the summer we could eat outside wherever we wanted; usually it was close by and there was always an extra mouth at the table. In the winter it was sports with me and my dad watching hockey, the Olympics or whatever. The house always had the same smell to it on Saturdays, just like it did at Christmas and with its own ambiance. Sometimes now, I can almost get there again if we have hamburgers and the mood is just right. Don't sit there like you don't know what I'm talking about. Tell me some of you don't have the same moments. Try this: think of a time when you were a kid when you felt the best and happiest. When you looked forward to those days because they felt so good—that's what I'm talking about. I won't lie, I might consider giving up a testicle for one day like that again. Who wouldn't right? Nah, I aint giving up one of the boys for anything.

My dad thought he was Grizzly frigging Adams and tried to prove this to us by taking us on camper excursions all over the countryside. One day when I was very young he showed up with a beat-up old camper and proudly showed it off to us like he'd gone out and shot it himself. This thing wasn't pretty but it was his and he loved it. Pops was all about family time, and this was his answer to doing more of it. We would load up every summer for our two weeks on the road and off we would go. I was never privy to the itinerary; I just got out and help set up wherever it was we landed. I was the official trailer-backer-upper. It was my job to guide my dad and his pride and joy into whatever slot we were destined to inhabit for the next few days. The trick here was to get it right the first attempt, at the most the second. If you couldn't manage that little task, you were replaced by Mom, who at the frustration of my dad, seemed to get endless attempts. Once in the slot it was hooking up the water, sewer (Hated that job. Always got something nasty on me.) and power, if available. Now that's roughing it. The closest we got to being an episode of survival was having to walk a few yards to the communal showers and shitter. Lastly, the trailer had to be leveled and this, boys and girl, was a major undertaking and only performed by Mr. Adams himself and his OCD misguidance. It could take hours and sometimes required multiple tweaking events.

At some point—I think it was a birthday present—I acquired a pup tent. This was set up at every place we stopped and lived in for the duration. Not only was it my house to have as I saw fit, it became the portable fort for all the kids we met and played with at these campsites. I got my first kiss from a girl in that tent and have no idea who she was—didn't really care either, I reckon. It also allowed me the freedom

15

of getting up every morning at the crack and going fishing all by myself.

I have a shitload of memories from these trips but this particular flashback sticks out like a rooster's dick in a hen house. We had cooked some stuff on the grill for supper one night and somehow forgot to take all the extra meat off the grill, a big no-no because bears like that shit. It's like going to their house and asking them to join you for dinner, and this time was no exception. I'm all snuggled away in my sleeping bag in the pup tent when I hear something outside the tent and it's breathing loud and hard. I hear the grill get knocked over and whatever this is pushing it around. By now, I have figured out what is going on and I'm thinking it's coming for me next as soon as it gets a whiff of me and the shorts I'm about to shit in. Here is the dumb part. I eased out of my sleeping bag and out the flap of the tent and ran for the camper like my ass was on fire and my hair was catching. Shit! The door was locked, so I kept running all the way to the lake and into the water. Now I'm neck deep in the water with nothing on but my tighty whiteys with my 8 year old reasoning being that the bear wouldn't go in the water. I am glad I never had that theory tested because I would have lost due to this little tidbit: they not only can swim, but they can kill shit while they're doing it, a fact I was not educated on at the time. It apparently didn't care about me because he took off as soon as my dad opened the camper door and started shouting. He was done anyway; he got his dinner, was probably already full and couldn't eat another bite. Dad was laughing his ass off and in the years to follow, he took great delight in recounting this moment of terror in my life to anyone who would listen. All bullshit aside, I had some of the best times of my young life on these camper excursions. Even though the car ride took a little out of you, the prize at the end of the day was more than worth it.

In our house there were two cars. One was a Pontiac Parisian we took when we had to go somewhere important or Pops went to work; the other was an ugly pale green Rambler station wagon. This was the family mule and it hauled kids, groceries, skis, more kids, hockey gear, dogs, camping gear, and more kids . . . yada yada. It was a great car and the best part was we got to ride in the back with the window down so we could throw shit out and make faces at the people behind us.

'Course if we got caught it was our ass, but worth it for the laughs. I mostly rode back there 'cause dad and his cigarettes were up front. We took this thing to drive-in movies, hauled the camper and we even got to sleep in it on camping trips. It had one of those childhood smells that if I come across it today it takes me right back to that car and all the associated nostalgia. Unlike the Parisian, you could spill something in it and make a mess without too much of a repercussion, but the Parisian—holy shit that was the Taj Mahal of cars at our house. You had to be de-loused and all kids spotless to get in that beast. We were filthy little kids so we stayed mostly delegated to the Rambler, which was more fun anyway.

When the cars got dirty it was up to me and Steve to wash them. I really hated that chore because Pops was such a sticky bastard on the details with the Parisian and it had to be pristine. I always wanted to take a leak in the back seat, close it up for a few hours and let that summer heat go to work. Of course I wouldn't be sitting here talking to you right now, but somehow I would love to have seen my dad's face just before he knocked me the fuck out. Chores were a big deal in our house. Animals had to be fed, lawns had to be cut, cars washed, leaves raked and dog shit to be picked up, just to mention a few.

The thing I never quite grasped as a kid was procrastination. Boy, I found every reason in the world not to do shit, then ended up having to do it in a hurry and usually under the threat of John Paul (my grandfather) or Pops kicking my ass. If I had just got whatever it was done, I wouldn't have been yelled at or threatened. Nope, not me, always had to do things the hard way. It's funny because I said the same things to my kids growing up, and it didn't make any difference to them either. According to my dad, chores built character and taught you responsibility. I thought it was just cheap child labor. When I got about 6 years old I started getting an allowance of 25 cents. Now don't laugh, that was a shit-load of money to a kid at that age. I would get my allowance on Saturday and walk into town, usually with my brother and sister in tow, and get into the movies and some kinda candy for that quarter. Man, back then you could let your kids out of your sight to do this kinda thing. You wouldn't dream of doing it now, would you?

That, my friends, is the world we have allowed it to become. What a shame.

If I wanted anything as a kid, like a toy or something special, I had to work for it by asking for extra chores and getting paid to do them and saving up. My dad would usually match half of the cost if he felt it was worthy; otherwise I was on my own. First thing I ever bought on my own was a K-tel greatest hits LP and I played the damn grooves off that thing. You know, a record—it went round and round on a record player? Some of you have no idea what I'm talking about, so Google it. The biggest venture I ever went in on with my Pops was a red Flyer wagon that I hitched to the back of my bike, and I had to come up with a whole $7 for! The bike wasn't actually mine; it was my dad's hand-me-down Raleigh Racer. It was a big-ass heavy red monster; if I dropped it I had some work ahead of me getting it upright. I had to have wooden blocks on the pedals for a few years 'cause I couldn't reach the pedals and kept slamming my nuts on the cross bar and guys, I'm here to tell you that gets real old after a while. Because it was so big I had to have about 20 feet of clear runway to get off and on the thing, and it hauled ass once I got it moving.

Summer time as a kid wasn't always just screwing around, playing and doing whatever; at times it got semiserious. I had a friend named Scott that lived next door and his dad was a full blooded Sioux Indian. The summer I met Scott I was probably about age 10, and his dad decided that because we liked camping and fishing, he would teach us how to survive in the woods and track animals the way they did with his ancestors. Scott already knew a lot of this but he did it with me anyway. His dad could track a 4 day old fart if you needed him to. This guy was real good, and I learned a lot about plant medicine, tracking and laying traps, what to eat and not to eat, direction in the woods and a bunch of other very useful things. I don't hunt animals—criminals yes, animals no. I just can't bring myself to kill an animal unless I need to eat, but I went with Scott and his dad, who hunted with a bow and traps. We stayed out in the woods once for five days and had only what we caught and found, and it was freaking awesome. Unfortunately, it is a perishable skill to some degree and if you don't practice regularly you're going to lose some of it, and I have. I am still very comfortable in the wilderness and I suppose if push came to shove, I would remember enough to get me home.

School for the most part sucked the big one. Teachers, bless their hearts, have the most obnoxious job ever of putting up with little shits like me that grow up to be bigger shits. It's more than anyone should have to bear. I was one of the most obnoxious kids in school. Trouble with a capital "T". I didn't kill or maim anyone; however, there was this one kid by the name of Phillip Butler who by all standards and reasoning of my young mind needed killing—a prick of a kid who was bigger than most and like all bullies got the greatest delight in picking on other kids smaller than him. It all came to a head with him and me in grade 6 the day before school let out for the summer. He had been picking on my little brother and mouthing me off several days prior to this soooooo . . . It was him, me, playground and school house rules. Now this wasn't the last time I would come away from a fight with my ass whooped but I gave as good as I got and as John Paul was always fond of reminding me, "When you are losing, fight dirty." A couple of weeks later I saw Butler coming down the street on his bike so I picked up a stick, waited for him to come by, then wham! I threw the stick into the spokes of his front wheel. The rest, as they say, is history, my friends.

From about grades 3 through 8 I seem to have always been in some kind of confrontation with some asshole or another. Often it was over something as stupid as "I don't like your face." I will say this, though, I was rarely the instigator but buddy, if they wanted to dance I was the guy to ask. I never said no to a good throw-down, even though this way of life was a never-ending source of pissed off to my mom because I often tore up my good school clothes. What got on her last nerve, I think, was she couldn't do or say anything much if it was justified in the defense of my siblings. My little brother got me into a lot of it. He would shoot his mouth off and then tell them, "Oh yeah, well, my brother can beat you up!" Thanks Steve, appreciate it. The other side to this was the rule my dad had. "If you don't stick up for your brother and sister you will answer to me when you get home." By now y'all know what that meant. Nonetheless, I grew up being pretty handy with my fists, even though I was never very big, usually the smallest in the bunch, and I think that just made my attitude worse. The whole "fuck you, let's do this" attitude instead of taking the high road in hindsight probably wasn't the smartest choice but you know, I wouldn't change anything 'cause life is the best teacher out there.

Besides the scrapping, school to me was just a daily pain in the ass and in hindsight I probably was a little on the ADD side, so after the first hour or two I was ready to move on to bigger and better. The problem with this thinking was they didn't give a shit what I wanted. I was just one of about 30 other piggies in the class, so this just created the need for me to entertain myself in the form of spitballs, elastic band guns and Green Hornet water pistols that were just some of the modes of entertainment in my world. Bubble gum was a banned item, but it was like prison; you could always seem to find some to leave stuck to the bottom of some desk. Remember that shit? If there were 40 desks in the room, you always managed to get the one with gum stuck to the bottom of the seat, and it always smelled like someone had just taken a dump in the desk. I had one desk on the first day of school that smelled so bad when I sat down that I looked in the desk for a body left behind from the previous year. No body, but there was what I thought to be a 6 month old baloney sandwich and something that might have passed as a petrified shit-filled diaper. I never really was able to give it a positive identification but it wasn't moving so that was good.

That's another thing. You ever notice that elementary and junior high schools have their own smell? They range from "oh my God, what the fuck is that smell" to "gee, that doesn't smell too pleasant but my eyes aren't watering." I have my own theory on this. Besides kids just being unsanitary, filthy little mongrels at this age, with smells even a bloodhound would balk at, there was the cafeteria.

In my day this place just frigging stunk; I mean like it could knock a buzzard off a shit wagon kinda stink. Even today in hospitals I work in, if I smell something that smells like a cross between someone's nasty ass and seven day old road kill coming from the cafeteria, I'm not eating there. I've worked at this one hospital for over seven years and have never set foot in the cafeteria because of the fucking smell emanating from it. Let's be honest here, if they served you the same shit on a shingle today that they gave you in the school cafeteria, would you eat it? Hell no, you wouldn't. You'd be wanting your money back and someone's ass would be getting a chewing, right? Of course, there are always those of you who could and would eat shit that would gag a goat, and y'all aren't included in this current conversation.

Kids never noticed the smell but I'm sure our parents got several whiffs but were too polite to say anything and just figured this was what kids smell like because we all smelled the same, right? We typically smelled like old piss, wet dog, dirt, food, ass or a combo of any of the above. A few years back I went to my daughter's class for a Father's Day deal and damn, those kids had some funk; then I went to my grandson's class not too long after and guess what? Same smell. I don't know if this is a hereditary smell being passed on through generations but it is always the same. Nothing else comes close to smelling like it, either.

School always had the traditional breaks in the school year. You know, thanks giving, Christmas, MLK, Easter and the odd shorter day off here and there, called "professional days". I found out later, when I taught high school for a while, that "professional day" was really just code for "I need a break from these little bastards" day. No shit, that's a true fact—ask a teacher if you don't believe me. Every kid looked forward to these breaks, everyone except Tony. This dumbass must have had an apartment hidden away in the gym or somewhere, because he was always at school. He was a member of just about every club there was and never played any sports. You know the guy I'm talking about because every school has at least one. He/she was usually the smartest fucker in the village and also the biggest nerd. This of course dictated, according to wilderness law, that a chosen few of us hunted them on a daily basis to give them the required wedgie.

For me Christmas was the holiday I could not wait for. Not just 'cause we got outta school but because in our house it was the most special of times. Christmas at our house was just cool because we didn't have a lot, but we had each other. Our family spent a great deal of time with each other over these holidays because that was what it was about to us. Mom made all kinds of goodies, including her famous Christmas cake. I say famous 'cause over the years I have known survivors who have tried it and love it to the point that every year they ask for some. You want to put some weight on? Eat a few pieces of this cake; you'll be running around like the fat bastard on an Austin Powers movie. My favorite was the mince tarts. They were to frigging die for folks. If I had less control I would be 400 lbs with diabetes from eating Mom's goodies.

My brother and I shared a room growing up and it got a little ugly at times, I'm not kidding. Fight? Hell ya we fought, all the damn time. The room was divided in half and the rules were simple: don't touch my shit and I won't beat your ass. At Christmas time we had a kind of truce and went more by the Geneva Convention war rules. There was always someone in the house visiting, the tree was up, and decorations were everywhere, candles lit, and an ambiance you could not buy with all the money in the world. In places we lived where we had snow, that just made it all the better. Christmas Eve was hard to take sometimes because as a kid, you just wanted the fat man to show up, drop off your shit and get lost. We had stockings and the rule was that we stayed in our rooms until Mom and Dad got squared away, then it was a sprint to the tree to seize our plunder. Every Christmas we picked someone and made a present. It didn't have to be the holy shit of creations—just something. If you didn't make something, you had to do something nice for them. We were allowed to open one present on Christmas Eve. Of course, we'd always go for the big, heavy shit so my parents got smart and didn't put the good stuff out till we went to bed. Then it would all show up under or around the tree like the fat man brought it. That's the story they gave us, anyway.

I don't know that I ever bought the whole Santa Claus thing, anyway. Why? Because I tracked down most of the presents before they hit the tree, that's why. There are only so many places adults can hide stuff. My dad got smart, though, and started keeping it at work. When you tell a kid not to go in the shed, what do you think they're gonna do? I remember being about five or six and listening to the radio when they had this running spiel on local radio about the airport tracking Santa's sleigh on the radar. According to the guy on the box, Santa and his sleigh should have been over my house in full view at least twice. Never saw him. I got up on the roof the next morning and nothing—no tracks, boot prints, sleigh marks or reindeer shit to be found. That pretty much clinched it for me. So although I never believed it, I did my best to make my kids believe it. A little payback, maybe.

My parents always had a grownup party every New Year's, which was code for "let's get all fucked up." It was great for us because we got to stay up as long as we wanted or till the last partier left, whichever came first, and eat all the junk food we could get our hands on. 'Course as much as we tried, none of us ever made it to midnight; most years we'd be out cold before. We got better at it as we got older. The rule was stay away from the grownups. We never did that, of course; we always found a way to spy on them somehow. Most of the time there were other kids staying over with us because their parents were getting shitfaced with mine. With any luck one of them was a girl or one of my friends. I hated New Year's. I hated it 'cause I knew Christmas was almost over and it would be back to school and the start of another year. The first part of any year always seemed so blah to me 'cause there was nothing really to look forward to except the summer. I didn't know until later in my medical career that kids have the most behavior and academic problems in school in the months of January-March. That's cause it fucking sucks, that's why—ask anyone in school; they'll tell you.

Around grade eight we become much more aware of how we look and smell, the clothes we wear, the number of zits on our face and even the language we use—'cause why? Hormones, that's why, and more specifically the sexual connotation of these hormones with the opposite sex. This, my fellow cave dwellers, is a major physical and social adaptation and not to be dealt with lightly. I never really got the birds and the bees speech from my parents; all my dad said on the subject was try not to act like an asshole and use a condom. Thanks Dad, another father-son session leaving me totally prepared to face the world. By this time we . . . well I, was well aware that my pecker had metamorphosed into a divining rod for the female gender; what I wasn't sure of was why. I was pretty sure it couldn't be just for self-amusement. Playing cowboys and Indians, frog hunting and other trivial child-like behavior, although fun, no longer was as relevant as the cute blond girl two rows over. It became so important that in grade nine I took home economics class instead of shop, to the amazement and the jealousy of the other guys in my class when they figured out there ain't no girls in shop. Hell, I even learned to sew some and do a little work on the stove, but it never carried through into adulthood, folks, because I can't cook for shit. Even my dogs have turned down my culinary products and that should tell you all you need to know right there. Fade to my first school dance and a girl named Sherry.

This bitch broke my heart. She might as well have just killed me and got it over with 'cause that's what I felt like at 11 years old. She was in my homeroom and math class and was God's answer to twelve year old girls with no tits. What did I know about tits then? Nothing really, other than they came in different sizes and, according to Dad's Playboys, were nice to stare at for hours. What I did notice was Penny, who sat behind her, had enough titty for both of them and several others.

Not to go off topic, but allow me this digression because this had always been an enigma and a source of deep reflection to me growing up. My apologies to the women because this next little bit is more directed to the boys in the crowd. Why were not all women created equal in the titty department? As with most things, the answer came with age. The answer being this, oh fellow male chauvinists: then we males would have nothing to stare at and allow imaginations to runneth over about and further, it gives women another weapon to use upon us. If they were all the same we wouldn't ogle at them because we already know what's under the hood. No, the Creator was a genius in that this keeps the male species wondering and drooling.

Sherry was my first crush. I thought the world revolved around her and I was just along for the ride. She knew this too, and true to female form made me work for it. Unlike the extrovert you see before you today, I was very shy and just her even talking to me would bring me close to pissing myself. It took weeks of practicing what I would say and trying to act cool the whole time, but I finally asked her to go to a school dance and she agreed. This is where a little planning probably would have been beneficial. I show up to the dance and it dawns on me that I can't dance—not a frigging step that could pass for dancing, anyway.

What a dumb ass. So here's what I did . . . nothing, not a damn thing. I didn't even really talk to her 'cause I didn't know shit about talking to girls either. The next thing I know she and Wayne are dancing to a slow song and I'm out. I can't blame her either, because she went to the dance with a block of wood and according to adolescent ruling if you can't do shit, ya don't get shit. What is amazing to me is how things like this scar a kid's psyche 'cause even today when I hear the song that they were dancing to, I go straight there like it was yesterday. I don't cry and whine like I did then, but you get the picture. As with all young men and women, there were a string of hearts broken and stomped on for several years onward. Little did I know, this was just a preview to other events, heartaches and scars to my soul that were to reveal themselves on my path to maturity.

THE ARROGANCE OF ADOLESCENTS

I mentioned earlier my dad was in the military and this meant moving a lot. He would get posted to different units in different states and countries and we would have to follow after him. For a while I was never in the same school more than one year in a row. At one point we were posted to Lahr, Germany and brother, what a ride that turned out to be. Southern white trash lands in Germany—not good for the Germans at all. This part of my life, although clear in memory, is a little foggy in its presentation. By this I mean I have a clear recollection of what happened, just not necessarily in the correct time line, but what the hell, here goes.

Germany was a unique place to be a teenager in. The drinking age over there is 14 and their beer is 10-14% alcohol. Already we're ahead of the game, right? Not yet, my friends, not yet. There was also something called "Schnapps". These little shots were some of the worst mind benders one could ever inflict on one's self. The one you are probably familiar with in the USA is Jagermeister (pronounced yeager miseter). Should have been called Yack miseter. That shit could make Deep Throat gag and it was probably the more pleasant of the schnapps. Others were probably designed and used by the Nazi SS for interrogation in WW II. There are a few rules to drinking in Germany. Rule one: Don't mix these two. It's either the beer or the Schnapps, not both. Rule two: Don't mix schnapps. Pick one and stick to it. Rule three: Have a spare set of clothes stashed because the ones you're wearing are going to need burning. If you don't heed rules one and two, you run the risk of irreversible brain dysfunction. (That should have been on the label) There is no telling how smart I would have been if I stayed home on those nights I have no memory of. The ones I spent crawling in the bedroom window drunker than Cooter Brown (a real guy by the way) after puking all over someone's front lawn. To be honest, there were several nights I have no recollection of. Of the three years we were there, I reckon I spent a total of a month of it fucked up in some form or another and spent another 14 months in the hospital trying to learn to walk again.

I had a part time job working in a warehouse on the military base making a whopping $1.72 an hour and back then, my friends, it was big money to me. Anyway, long story short, I fell off a pallet about 10 feet and landed on a cobblestone floor flat on my back. It hurt like a sum-bitch but I started to feel better after a while and went back to work. I went camping with some friends the weekend after the fall and it still bothered me but we got shit-faced and all was well with the world. It kept bothering me and getting worse after a month so I finally went to the doctor. They took some x-rays and said I just pulled a muscle and to quit being a pussy. (He didn't say that but I bet he thought it.) The pain just gets worse over the next several weeks and one day I'm going up the school steps and bam! My legs give out and I can't move them like normal, almost not at all, and I definitely had issues with feeling them. You can imagine the sphincter tone on this moment; well actually, I had no sphincter tone—that went with the legs. They haul my ass to the hospital and that is where I pretty much spent the next almost year and a half.

Apparently when I fell at work I must have broken my back a little and just to make bad worse, when I was camping after the accident I drank un-pasteurized milk. This, I am told, set me up for Tuberculosis of the spine, also known as Potts disease. The school event was my back finally coming apart and breaking. Back then, medical advancements were not what they are today. They told my mom and dad, "He's not going to walk right, if at all, again." Now folks, my family has a certain tenacity that is a plus most times but can be detrimental in others. We don't give up and we practice the ole "I don't give a shit what you say" attitude. This time it worked in my favor because my dad decided that this doctor was full of shit and set out to prove it. Without the aid of things like cell phones or the Internet, he eventually found Dr Norman

Shaw in Manchester, England, who had dealt a lot with this, and he is the reason I walk upright and don't drag my knuckles today. An added bonus was the hospital I was in was just down the street from where my mom grew up so we had some relatives there sponge off and terrorize.

Basically what Dr. Shaw did was remove two ribs out of my left side and graft them into my spine where it was tore up so it became fused. I spent just under a year in a body cast that went from my ankles to my neck. I shit through a hole in the back and pissed through one in the front. They would come and flip me over four times a day so I could stare at the bottom of the bed instead of the ceiling. As you might have surmised, I could not reach my own butt to wipe it so it was tasked to the nursing staff, bless their hearts. The dexterity of the task was totally dependent on which way my ass was pointed at the time, so if I was face up, the nurse doing the honors looked like she was under there changing the oil. Probably not what most 14 year olds were doing at that stage of their lives, I'm sure, but as a plus side to all this I had the best grades ever in school while I was in the hospital—go figure.

The day I got the cast off I walked 11 steps to the shitter and took my first pee standing in almost a year. I was discharged home a few weeks later and fitted with this steel brace that I had to wear whenever I was up and mobile. It's hard to describe this thing but basically it had 2 steel rods that ran up my back on either side of my spine, with straps that went around my shoulders and around my abdomen. I grew to hate this thing with a passion but it was part of me for two years and a necessity I didn't really fathom then. I sure didn't want more surgery, so I dealt with it. My friends thought it was funny as hell to hang me off a door hook from this thing. I guess boys are just that—boys. On top of all this, for another two years I had to take anti-tuberculin medicine that tasted like shit and made me nauseated. Why do people say "It tasted like shit"? Saying this would imply you had eaten shit prior and were able to make that comparison. Just a thought.

I am most grateful and humbled by all that was done for me. It was a small amount of time to give up compared to what I have been able to accomplish due to the care I received. To Dr Shaw, for your skilled hands and patience, cheers mate! To the doctors that scared my parents to death telling them I would be an invalid the rest of my life . . . kiss my ass.

Y'all probably know this but Europe has some of the best skiing in the world. Well, just before we were posted to Germany my parents decided they needed to be rid of the kids on the weekends so they signed us up for skiing lessons. This is the only sport I ever saw my brother do that he liked and was fairly good at. They start by teaching you to do the "snow plow". This is where you point the tips of the skis together and hope they don't cross while at the same time digging in the inside edges. Kinda like the way Jerry Lewis used to walk in his movies. It was hard at first but got easier the more you did it. As usual that just wasn't going to cut it for me and I worked like hell at this till soon enough I was able I move on to parallel skiing. This is where you keep both feet tight together and sort of slide your back end around by shifting you weight left and right. Enough of the ski lesson. We get to Germany and lo and behold, they have a ski team at the school so of course, yours truly signed his ass up. This worked out just fine until the back thing came along and that got put on the back burner for a while. Anyway, we were able to go on a good number of ski weekends with the school and brother, it was a non-stop party most of the time. There was some serious drinking and girl hunting on these weekends, and as an added bonus I even learned some skiing, too. It was because of these weekend excursions I actually became one of the best around in my age and was able to get into some trick skiing and ski ballet for a while. I have been graced enough to have skied in about every country in Europe that has any kinda hill in it and loved every minute of it.

Every year the school scheduled a "Ski Week" for grade 9 and above, which was kinda the spring break of Europe. What a blast, skiing all day and partying all night. We were supposed to be behaved and to mind but we didn't so we took our punishment and kept on like the arrogant little bastards we were. Guys, being the way they are in front of the female species, tend to work harder at being good at something if girls are paying attention to it so we can show off just that much more, and ski week was just that—who was the best at showing off. In my class it was one of my better friends, Brendon. I was sure this guy could ski on one leg and at the same time be doing his homework and laundry and never miss a beat. No matter how hard I tried, I was never that good. On top of this he was a good-looking guy, so you can guess how this went for him. We all just lined up like dogs looking for a bone to catch whatever girl he didn't want. There was a sort of test at the end of the week to see how much you had improved, depending on your skiing level. The test was a timed descent down the hill in whatever conditions the hill and weather presented that day. Of course, Brendon always won the thing—just what he needed: more things for the girls to be in love with.

It has been years—well, more like decades—since I strapped on skis and I do miss it. It's one of those things that you never get around to doing but think about it all the time. Seems like a lot of things go that way as you get up in years. As a side note, 6 months after I got out of the hospital I was back on the skis and won the competition for my age and I even managed to beat Brendon by 3 whole seconds.

Being teenage male chauvinists, conversations would inevitably come around to subject of girls and who had gotten laid and who hadn't. I hadn't and it sucked because as any guy will attest to, we are an insurmountable hill of hormones at this age, especially when it came to our quest to conquer the opposite sex. I was 14 when I lost the ole cherry. The problem with this major life event is I barely remember it because I was way, way fucked up at the time. This is why I don't drink German Schnapps anymore, because I would like to remember at least some of the monumental milestones in life as I truck along. Same goes for tequila, but that is another story we'll get to in just a little bit. All I can tell you is that Dennis, my best friend, and I were out doing the town again as always, when we ran up on these two German girls. I say girls only because I know she had a vagina and Dennis said his did too. I have vague images of their faces and I'm pretty sure I got the ugly one, but Dennis would never tell me. We went to someone's house and I threw up outside the door before we went in, which I felt was very thoughtful of me not to do in the house. I'm sure the girl appreciated the essence of fresh vomit on the guy she was about to do the horizontal mamba with but apparently it wasn't a deal breaker for her. I knew this was not her first time because she seemed to know what she was doing and what she was after, while I had no clue. What I knew came from porn movies and Playboy.

There's really not much to tell you from this point other than it was over in about 10 minutes; we went our way and they went theirs. Slam—bam, thank you ma'am. The good thing about this event in hindsight was it could only get better from this point on. I mean really, when you start in the gutter it's only up from there, right? I have no idea who she was, her name, age, nothing, and I never saw her again. Dennis and I went back to the place we found them a few times to see if we recognized anyone or they us. Negative. I'm just glad my pecker didn't fall off. I always wished my first time had been in the back of a car. I have no idea why I think that, just do. It was not to long after this easily-forgotten juncture in my manhood that we lost Pops.

My dad always told us, "If something happens to me the commanding officer and a chaplain will be at the door and I won't be coming home again" and that's exactly how it went, folks. My mom, aunt Vinnie and I were home when they showed up and naturally, my mom lost it. That tends to happen when you lose your best friend, husband and the father of your kids. At some point it became my mission to locate and inform my younger brother and sister as to the bad news. I really don't recall where my sister was, I think at a friend's house, and my brother had gone to see *Jaws* at the movie theater. To this day I can't see that movie without going through it all again. I guess telling them was really the only thing I stepped up and did for my mom during the whole shitty scenario. In my defense, what the fuck did I know about being a leader or being a pseudo-father figure to my siblings? I was just really a kid myself. A self-centered teenager to be exact, complete with zits, and I did not have the age, wisdom or experience to answer the questions posed to me, nor the know how to act like an adult in a kid's body.

The fact that I had been somewhat spoiled by my stint in the hospital before he died just made it worse. I didn't know then what I know now, or I could have kicked my own self in the nuts. Regardless, I did not act like I should have nor took the responsibilities I should have to lessen the load for Mom. In a word, I was a dick. I had a girlfriend at the time and put all my emotional focus into her and me instead of the family I should have. The shrinks call that a form of "emotional transference"; I call it being an asshole and the truth of it is I didn't try hard enough and I have no excuse for my behavior. Needless to say, the next year or so did not go well with my mom and me and finally, at the ripe old age of 16, I left home to be on my own and have been ever since but for brief interludes where I re-entered the fold for some reason or another.

My first car was a Toyota Corolla. I loved that car, and the reason was because I built the sum-bitch by myself. I went to the junkyard and got two identical cars and spent the winter and spring of my sixteenth year building one out of two. It looked like shit, drove like shit and probably even smelled like shit, but it was mine and I was proud of it. It had a cheesy-ass cassette player that had a fetish for eating every other tape and the heater worked when it felt like it, mostly in the summer—never could figure that out. I had redneck air conditioning and the floor leaked when it rained, which really was not a big problem unless you were on a date. True to my redneck ingenuity, I cured that problem with double rubber door mats. I thought that I was Richard frigging Petty in this thing. I drove the piss out of it to the tune of a quart of oil about once a week. Most of the time I had bad tires on it and didn't think this was a problem in my immature adolescent, selfish mind until the night I lost control and had been drinking.

In everyone's lives there is that "oh shit" moment that you got by with on the skin of your teeth and could not even fathom how your life would have been if had been worse or gone the other way. Well, here is one of mine, ladies and gents. I was about seventeen and the world, I believed, revolved around me and nothing could or would go wrong because I was super teenager! Well it did, and it scared the piss out of me. I had been out partying at this club and was about half in the bag and instead of doing the right thing like acquiring alternate transportation, I climbed into the Mario Andretti machine with about 4 of my friends and proceeded to drive like a total asshole. As I mentioned prior, good tires were not a priority at this point, it was raining, and I'm stupid. I lost control and slid across the lane, just missed another car coming the other way and drove right into a lamppost at about 50mph. The car was totaled but somehow no one was hurt except me. I had some cuts, a few bruises, and some sticky brown stuff in my shorts. I have no idea why the cops didn't arrest me; they had to know I'd been drinking, but they didn't and all I got was a ticket for careless driving and a ride home. Thank God no one was hurt or killed. To this day, folks, I am compulsive about my vehicle maintenance and do not drive if I have had a few. I have a scar on my left shoulder from that night and even today when I notice it I still feel so grateful it was not worse and guilty for what I put others through out of my own stupidity. I have had two car accidents in my life and the other one was nowhere near my fault so that makes the score 1:1 and I would like it to stay that way.

I guess I started to grow up, or at least I tried to, and a year or so went by before I got myself in some big-time hot water. I'd like to tell you it wasn't entirely my fault but the fact is, I made some stupid decisions and was arrogant enough to believe I wasn't wrong. The whole world was out of step except me type of stupid arrogance. In my defense, nothing was intentional, more like happenstance, but it put me on a path that would set the tone for the rest of my life. It came the hard way, as usual, but it was a lesson and experience I am most grateful for.

MARTIAL ARTS

The Journey

At one juncture along my merry way, I didn't make the soundest decisions about what to do or what I was doing. I was just young—around 18, I think—when I made one of the worst decisions of my life . . . and also the best one. Bear with me, please, because I'm going to get to this one the long way around.

At the time I worked for this drilling company in a little town in the middle of pump handle nowhere. After work one day we decided to blow off some steam and went to the local watering hole for a few cold ones. I left half in the bag a few hours later on my way to meet with one of the opposite sex. As I was going across the parking lot I saw a guy with a girl pinned against a pickup truck, just whaling the shit out of her. Being the knight in shining armor I believed myself to be at the time, I went in for the assist, as any chivalrous dumb shit would do. The long and short of it was this guy and I ended up going at it and at one point he grabbed a 2x4 out of the truck and came at me. We locked up and the next thing I know, I am beating this guy half to death. I feel someone grab me from behind and so I think in my rage someone else wants a piece of this so I will oblige them. Trouble with that decision was that someone was a cop. This is the first of only two times I would be seriously involved with the police and neither had anything to do with something I had done . . . well, sort of. I hit the cop hard twice before I figured out what was going on, but by then it's way too late. Two other cops have me face down on the ground, a foot on my neck and cuffed. Of course, the alcohol on board didn't help with my decision-making skills; that, combined with my big mouth and temper, just kept digging a bigger hole to get myself dropped in. I get to the jail and put in the cell with several others and one native Indian who decided he didn't like this white man's face, so it was on again like Custer's last stand. The jailers come in and separate us, I get taken to a solitary cell where they decided I needed another lesson in etiquette. This I did not listen to, either, and hit one of them.

So, to summarize, in a matter of a few hours I fought a guy with a 2x4, a cop, an Indian and a jailer. Why? Cause I'm an idiot, and for what? So I could save the damsel in distress? This shit gets better, my friends. They hold me over the weekend with no bail because I assaulted a police officer. When I finally get to court Monday morning the judge basically tells me "you're an asshole so you can be my guest here for the next month, until your case gets to court." Fan-fucking-tastic—all this over some asshole and his girlfriend and trying to do the right thing, with a healthy dose of my own stupidity thrown in for added fun. I could have just left them at it, but that's not how I was raised. I have integrity and standards, with rule #1 being: You don't hit women.

As court time finally rolled around, my lawyer informed me there had been more charges added to the original set. The girl and the guy have charged me with aggravated assault and basically said I started it and I was the one who hit the girl and came after him with the wood. What? Really!? So I go to court, the judge looks at my shining arrest record, listens to the only witness I had—whose story was exactly the same as mine, by the way—and says, "You're an asshole; here is 6 months to think it over." No shit, just like that, I was sentenced to 6 months in jail without even so much as a reach around. I was released 3 months later, after the judge was informed that the assault charges were perjured and total bullshit. Thanks, Lenny. (He was my attorney and not on the hate lawyer list.) The judge brings me into chambers, tells me I'm free to go and that this record will be expunged due to circumstances. Gee, thanks your Honor. So here I am, out of the "joint", per se, with absolutely nothing but what's in my pockets and on my back. My job and apartment were gone, as well some of my friends and of course, the girlfriend had moved on and I couldn't blame them either, really, 'cause who wants to be associated with a convicted felon, right? So what the fuck has this got to do with Martial arts? Wait, just bear with me a little longer; I am getting to it.

I stayed with a friend for a few days so I could get my shit together, or till his wife got tired of me lying on her couch. I finally decided to do the only thing I knew to do—go home. My mom lived on the other side of the country and I had about $30 to my name and what should have been a few days' excursion was almost 6 months in the making. I began hitchhiking my way and this, as I'm sure you are aware, is not a fast process. I ran out of money real quick and tried to keep going by doing odd jobs along the way. I had nowhere to stay so I parked my happy ass where ever I could: in barns, bus stops, abandoned houses, shopping malls, sheds and even a tree house for a few nights. I spent that next birthday cold, wet and hungry in a chicken coop in the middle of God knows where. I bet you're thinking that life was not at all that jolly for this young man, and you would be correct.

I was very fortunate to meet up with Sally and Bert at this point in my travels and the truth is, I'm not sure what direction I would have gone or even if I would be where I am today without the kindness of these people. They owned a little gas station and coffee shop in the middle of bum-fuck Egypt that I wandered up to one day looking for work, hungry, tired, filthy and looking like rolled shit. Bert took one look at me and said, "You ain't doing shit around here till you smell better," I stayed there cleaning tables, pumping gas, doing dishes, cleaning toilets and anything else that came up for about 2 months. I lived in the furnace/compressor/water heater room and was glad to have it because it was warm and dry. In their small way, they saved me by allowing me another path to be the person I am today. I say it that way because due to their kindness I believe I went the way I did and not another that could have been worse. It is also from them I learned the meaning and value of paying it forward. Gracias, Bert and Miss Sal, you are forever in my heart. I wish I had stayed in better touch, so if you guys ever read this, my email is on the cover. I know, I know, where is the martial arts part? Just gimme a minute.

Master Lee

The day I left Bert and Sally, they took me to a bus station in the city and dropped me off. The ride was a while leaving so I went across the street to the mall to kill some time. At one end there was a Taekwondo demonstration going on, where I saw this tiny little Oriental man jump in the air and do some things that just floored me. I was absolutely amazed. His name was Master Jun Kim Lee, at the time an 8th degree black belt, a direct family descendent of his martial art in Korea and soon to be one of biggest influences and mentors in my life.

I had done some martial arts training in the past but nothing that put me on the map as any kind of good or outstanding practitioner. I had never seen anyone as good as Master Lee or since, for that matter, in the art he practiced. I went up to one of the people with Master Lee and asked where his school was and was told he and the students were guests of a local dojo and were leaving today to back home. I got the address and went on my merry way. I made it home but the whole time I was there (three months) I kept thinking about this man and his extraordinary skill. He had a presence about him that just captivated me, so soon enough I left my mom's and went straight to this town, set up housekeeping, found a job and enrolled in his school. That was the beginning of the rest of my life.

My attitude was still rough and shitty at times—well ok, a lot of the time. I had to learn how to be a human again, sort of like the way a wild dog becomes domesticated. I studied hard and spent almost all of my free time at the dojo. Saturdays were the best class. In the morning Master Lee only taught the black belts and most of it consisted of sparring, and in the afternoon it was the junior belts that he taught personally. You had to be there on time because if class had started and you were late, tough titty, you were not allowed in. I would often make a day of it and bring breakfast and lunch with me so I could be there for both classes. It took me a little over 2 years to make red belt and after red is black. Lee did all the testing himself for red belt and above. There was no testing for lower belts because there were no lower belts; you were white till red. To confound the issue, there were no standards to the testing either. Each individual was differently tested; in other words, there was no getting ready for his test. You were ready when he said so and it was all based on merit, skill, attendance and his belief in you. One Saturday I'm getting all snuggled in to watch another black belt sparring massacre when Master Lee walks over to me and says,

"Put your Gi on and join the class." Now I'm freaking out and started thinking, *These guys are going to slaughter me. I'm not ready for this.* But you didn't say no to this man; there was too much respect involved. So, with my nut cup securely in place and the boys tucked inside, I join the class.

I would like to tell you that the practice of martial arts brings out the Zen in all people and there are no sadistic, mean ones out there but that would be bullshit, and that mine came in the form of Slay Turner. No, I'm not making that up; it's his real name: Slay. I am paired with him for drills and sparring and he had just gotten his black belt about 6 months prior. He was not without skills, especially in the leg department. I don't know what got into him that morning, but he proceeded to kick the hell out of me. He wasn't teaching me; he was trying to hurt me. I don't know why he was that way. I had spoken to him a few times—nothing out of the ordinary, just usual stuff—and he was about my age. Nonetheless, he was on a mission that morning. In the sparring part of class he went after me with a vengeance, and it was all I could do to keep him off me. The next thing I know, Master Lee stops the fight, tells me to sit down and faces off against Slay. I don't have to give you a narrative on how that went for him. He was asked to leave the class that morning and I saw him once more after that day, then not again for almost a year at an open tournament wearing another school's Gi.

I continued to go to the morning class, even though I was not a black belt, and never asked him why he brought me in. I just did as I was told. I progressed quickly and within 6 months I passed my black belt exam. This is when the learning began. I learned how to channel my aggressions and reign in my mouth and attitude (Well, kinda anyway). I was taught not only to be a student, but also to be an ambassador of the art and a mentor and teacher to those coming up. I really enjoyed teaching; there is a satisfaction like no other in seeing a student grow. Master Lee was not only my teacher, he was also my friend. His son Tyson (Ty to us) was a year younger than me but had been taught martial arts by his dad from the time he could walk, so that should tell you how good he was. Ty and I hung out a lot together and were friends, but it was always weird going to Master Lee's house. It was like entering a temple or some shit. I can't even begin to explain that feeling, folks, so you're just going have to guess at it.

Not too long after black belt testing, Master Lee told all the black belts that for the first time, Taekwondo was being considered for an Olympic event. In the next 6 months there were going to be tryouts for the possibility of being Olympic team members. There would be tournaments and selection for those who made our team, across the nation over the next year and a half. He wanted at least one of our school on that team if possible and of course everyone figured Ty as a shoe-in. He was by far the most talented and being the boss's son certainly was not a deficit. This, however, was not going to be the case; he had to earn it, as the rest of us did. Six out of the school, including me, tried out and this warranted and required extra and more intensive training from Master Lee. We were for the most part removed from regular classes, although we still had to teach. Lee would say, "It is a good way of seeing how much work you need to do on yourself. To teach you must know it more personally, not better than those you are teaching." Loved that quote. The workouts were focused, extremely intense, and this kind of work ethic earned me the world championship two years in a row.

Long story short, Bobby O (we called him Bobby "O" because no one could pronounce his last name except other Greeks) and I made the Olympic alternate team and Ty made the main team. There was a break in the training in this part of the story that involved Uncle Sam. I will explain later, but as it turns out it made no difference in the end. We were several months away from finding out if Taekwondo was going to be in the Olympics when Russia invaded Afghanistan. Guess who was sponsoring the Olympics? Russia! The peanut farmer in the white house, Jimmy Carter, decided that because of this outburst by the Russians we were going to boycott the games in protest—we being the good ole US of A. I don't remember getting that phone call asking if that was ok; they just made the decision for us. Since when does politics involve sports, asshole?! You didn't work your ass off and take several shit kicking's to get your spot on the team, now did you? We took it as was and went about our daily lives—what else could we do?

He never said it but Master Lee was very disappointed at the whole thing; you could tell it by his face and demeanor when he talked about it. As it was, a fight broke out between the ITA and WTA, the International Taekwondo Association and the World Association. The WTA and ITA were like a bunch of three year olds on even the simplest of things and they couldn't get along for shit. Taekwondo would not have another opportunity to be in the Olympics until it was a demonstration sport in Seoul in 1988 and then was officially recognized as medal event sport in 2000. Just for the record, I have never forgiven that motherfucker Carter, either. I don't give a shit how many houses he builds for the poor.

Master Lee and I parted ways about 6 months later, when another encounter with the law sent me on another path I was grateful for (ya, you read that right, grateful for). I stayed in touch with him as best as I could but I wish I had done better. He died in 1992 in a car crash, of all things, and his son took over the business. From what I heard it was never the same. Ty was good but didn't possess his dad's . . . what's the word . . . inner force and presence—something everyone who ever met him felt. The two federations continued to argue and fight well into the 1990s and I had moved on to bigger and better things, specifically Shorinji Ryu Kenkokan.

Shihan Kori Hisataka

I first came into contact with this martial art, Shorinji ryu Kenkokan, at a tournament in Baltimore that I gone to because it advertised full contact fighting with this odd looking gear called "Bogu" that covered your head and body. It was love at first fight and I proceeded to find out where all the schools were and began a practice and in-depth study that at the time of this writing has lasted over thirty-five years.

The art itself was not that old and was begun by Shihan Kori Hisataka in the 1920s. I won't bore you with details but it was a combination of jujitsu, judo, Shaolin Long hand fighting and Shotokan karate, and everything about it just fit very well with the way I fought and moved. I studied hard for a few years, quickly made black belt and from there began my own school that has continued to thrive with several generations of students as the owners and instructors for over 27 years. Even though I loved teaching I always felt that I was missing something, like having a gun but having bad aim and not knowing how to correct it. I wanted to really get a handle on this martial art so I decided that I needed to go to the source, Japan (Getting there is another story we'll get to), where Shihan Kori was, and also his son, 8th degree Masayuki Hisataka.

At the time I met Kori he was well into his 80s and not in the best of health. Regardless, he was still an imposing figure that demanded your attention and respect. The first time he came into the dojo I didn't even know he was there until everyone around suddenly stopped, kneeled and bowed toward the door where he was standing. Man, it was absolutely incredible to meet a living legend, something that would only happen once more in my life time, and really there are no words to describe this. We resumed class and he walked around looking at the students practicing their movements. When he got to me he said something to his son, but I have no idea what. Probably along the lines of "have we stooped so low as to let the Southern white trash in now"? I saw him just two more times before his death and both experiences are forever etched into my mind.

In time, I returned to the states a fourth Dan in shorinji ryu and the all-Japan champion. Masayuki took over from his father and things in the art and organization began to change, but not for the better, in my view. He was all about money and began changing some of the things his father had laid down as the basis for his style, the very reasons that had brought me 4000 miles to learn. The other side of him was very narcissistic and all about him wherever he went. Do not get me wrong, this man knew his shit. Masayuki is an exceptional martial artist and teacher; I just didn't gee haw with him personally and at times that made it a difficult environment to learn in.

Ueshiba Sensei

I lived in Japan several years and I was busy, with no lack of things to do. My desire to imbed myself in the Japanese martial arts was an obsession. (Ya . . . again) I began taking Aikido on my off days from Karate and fell in love with this art. It is very challenging to learn and practice and the most amazing thing to watch in the hands of a skilled practitioner. In my humble opinion and experience, there is nothing you can't defend yourself from with this art if you know your shit. It began with a man by the name of Sensei Morihei Ueshiba who believed, based on other martial arts, that there was a better way, a softer way, that was just as effective so he created Aikido. If you ever want to read about a fascinating man, pick up his biography; you will not be disappointed. As it is with most things, people have their own ideas on what should and should not be and Aikido was no exception. The art had some splintering early on and other forms of this art, such as Yoshikan Aikido, founded by Gozo Shioda, was one of them. This was not a turbulent split by any means. The art that Shioda taught remained rooted in Sensei Ueshiba's way and is as pure as its birth, but took a more self-defense posture in its teachings. In an interview before his death Shioda Sensei said, "Either you defeat your opponent or he defeats you. You cannot complain that he did not follow the rules. You have to overcome your opponent in a way appropriate to each situation." I studied under the students of Kisshomaru Ueshiba, Sensei's son, and his son Moriteru Ueshiba, who continued to teach at the original Aikikai dojo in Tokyo. I rarely saw him but his students that were my teachers were giving, knowledgeable and humble. It was here that I very briefly came under the instruction of the action movie star Steven Segal at a seminar he gave. By the way, that shit Segal fucks people up with in his movies is the real thing and he can do what you see him doing and a whole lot more. If you don't believe me and you want to find out for yourself, be my guest but bring a gun and shoot first.

Aikido has its roots in other martial skills, one prominently being the art of the sword (Katana), Kendo (Japanese fencing), Jodo (short stave) and Iaido (art of drawing and cutting with the sword). This is heavily emphasized in Aikido and one of the reasons I wanted to learn something that was not based just in hands and feet. I thought that learning a martial art based in only these weapons was the next logical progression with Aikido. I had heard of a guy who taught Kendo, Japanese fencing, and the other sword arts so I sought him out. I had no idea this decision would be another life event that would affect me so deeply it would alter me for the rest of my days.

Shimekake Sensei

This is where I met the second living legend as I mentioned earlier. Shimekake Sensei was eleventh generation samurai and a very un-imposing, kind, and physically deceptive man. At first glance, if you did not know Sensei and watched him dodder around the dojo, you might think you could whip this old man no problem. On that assumption you would be very wrong. You would have more problem than you wanted or could handle; trust me on this one. If you look up the original bad ass in the dictionary, it says "see him". Of the many times I faced off against Sensei in class, he would beat the shit out of me so bad I hurt for a week. If you put a Kendo Shinai (Bamboo Kendo sword) in his hands, he becomes a very, very bad dude.

It wasn't like I walked into Sensei's dojo and he said, "Welcome, come on in, sit down and take a load off"—far from it. The first day I went in I sat at the door for an hour waiting to be asked in. In Japan it's different than what we do here, you don't just walk in anywhere you please; there are protocols to be followed. Finally Sensei sent someone over to see what I wanted and they relayed the message that I wanted to start training and learning from him. His answer was a flat-out no. Sensei does not take Gaijin (white boys) as students but I was welcome to watch. This was not a racial slur on me; it is the Japanese way to stay within themselves, as they have done for hundreds of years. At first my feelings were a little bent but I got over it and decided I was going to keep trying.

Several times a week I went to the dojo and watched his classes and would ask again each time. After a couple of months, I walked in one morning and Sensei walked over to me and said something (I never did know what) and handed me what could only be described as a small log. It weighed a ton, was about 6 feet long, 3 inches across and made of teak. He walked me over to the corner and showed me this move where I raised it over my head and brought it down like you were cutting with a sword. He walked away and I did this for the whole rest of the class. At the end of class someone came to me and told me to be here again in the morning. So now I'm thinking I will finally be in the class, right? Wrong. I got there the next morning and several others over the next few months, to be re-united with the "log", and did the same thing all class.

I was late for "log class" one morning and when I got there I was taken to Sensei's little room off the dojo. I was sweating it because I'm thinking I'm gonna get the boot for being late, which in Japan is a huge sign of disrespect. Sensei sits me down and through his daughter, who spoke great English, wants to know all about me and why I stayed and worked with the log instead of quitting. I told Sensei my desire to learn from him was always greater than that of quitting. That must have been what he wanted to hear because Sensei asked me some more questions and told me to go home and be back in the morning. From that day on I was with Sensei almost constantly, it seemed, and if I could swing it, I was there daylight to dark. I think at one point he even tried to hook me up with his daughter but I slid out of that one before it got difficult. Sensei was incredible to watch and one of the best teachers I have ever had. It was from him I learned how to be a teacher and to be his friend.

I came to class one day and out of the blue Sensei says, "You teach class." These are the same guys that yesterday I was just another student with, but you did what Sensei said without question. I also knew him well enough to know that he had a hidden agenda in having me do this. My spoken Japanese was much better, thanks to my partying with the Yakuza that lived in my neighborhood and exposure in the dojo, so language and a lot of hand gestures got the job done. I thought at one point he was having me teach to amuse himself because he always had this grin on his face. I taught the classes several times a month and I never knew till I got there if I was student or teacher that day.

Before I knew it, the time came for me to go home. I had been there long enough, and I wanted to see my family. The week before I was to leave I went to the dojo as always, but when I walk in all is very quiet but for this Buddhist monk praying in a corner and what looked like the whole damn school sitting in front of this table with a Katana (Japanese Sword) on it. Now I'm thinking wtf? Someone die? Wedding? What? Two of the students come over and take me into this little room and start putting me put in this very formal kimono. They will not tell me what the hell is going on but whatever it is, it's important and has to do with me. I figure unless they're fixing to cut my head off I had just better go along with it and shut my pie hole.

I am taken back out into the dojo. Sensei is there in this very fine formal Kimono and he is standing in front of this table. I did not understand 100% of what he said to the school but it was basically telling them I was the eighth one ever to be named Sempi and the only white person in his 50 years of teaching. Sempi Ozo was the only one I knew of or had met. Translated, Sempi roughly means "Student teacher of the teacher". Now let me clarify something here, to put this in to a better perspective: the Japanese and their martial arts are and always have been a very strict and closed society that is traditionally only for the Japanese. For a white boy like me to be introduced into this line is highly irregular and very rare. It is not as uncommon now because of the number of martial artists that went to Japan to study but to be allowed this privilege back then was not the norm at all. Anyway, the monk comes over and starts praying over the Katana and me. Sensei picks it up and hands it to me and bows with his eyes to the floor. This is an honor I can't even begin to explain to you. This symbolizes his trust and faith in you and comes from older times of Iaido practitioners and samurai that when you bowed with your eyes down, you were trusting them not to kill you. The sword he hands me had been in his family for over 150 years. Traditionally when a Katana is given to a student by his teacher it is an acknowledgement that the teacher feels his Sempi is qualified to teach under him. The Katana is blessed in the Shinto way and given a new name by the new owner. In the old days the sword was usually new so it could start its own journey with its teacher. Shimekake Sensei named mine for me, again a great honor, and he called it "Ishogai", which means "For life". To this minute I have kept it and him very much in my heart for over 30 years.

Sadly, Sensei passed in 2000 of natural causes. I never really knew how old he truly was, but I'm betting at his death he was well into his nineties. His daughter told me Sensei taught classes all the way up until about a year before he died. His name, spirit, martial art and love will live in me as long as I draw breath. *Gambate Sensei, watashi wa anatawa ai shite.*

Kobura Dojo

After coming back from the land of the rising sun, I concentrated on teaching my students what I had learned. It was a difficult process at times because the Japanese Martial way and the way of Bushido is kind of like a religion, for lack of a better term, and is a foreign concept to most Gaijin. I had a few students that were the exception to the rule and I was able to get into them a small amount of what I had come to understand as a way of life. These few became my focus and my greatest pride, mostly because of their dedication to themselves, the art, the school and to me. I knew I was not going to be there for long; I had made plans to travel a different road and these dedicated few kept things moving forward long after I had left the picture. This story would not be complete without a few words on Bob.

Bob is and always will be, as close to me as any brother can be. He, without a doubt more than any other, is solely responsible for keeping the Kobura School open and my ambitions and hopes alive these many years. We met on my return from Japan when he was a white belt, and apparently he was somewhat nervous about our meeting. He kept hearing about this hard-ass teacher who'd been in Japan and now was coming back to take over the school. As he put it, "I got a little of the oh shit factor" about the whole thing. I had a reputation of being very thorough and hard on the students during training. Not in a bad way, just known for being very intense, dedicated and focused on being correct. Bob's whole thing was he was a white belt and not the most coordinated individual at that juncture of his life. It was really the first time in his life he had ever done anything like martial arts.

As a young man he had gotten himself in some trouble with the law that got him a few years in prison. While he was in there he educated himself and earned his degree. Upon getting out, he went to school to be a teacher and remains one today. He has a way with people that puts them at ease right away and from what his wife has told me, his students love him and I believe it because I love him, too.

Bob described himself to me once as "strong like bull, smart like street car". I don't believe that. He is a large man with a heart as big as all outdoors and as gentle as the breeze. His issue with martial arts was always a coordination problem, never heart—that he had plenty of. Finesse was not his strong suit but he worked harder and longer than anyone, with the same tenacity that got him back on the right track in prison. Today, he is Sensei at Kobura and has been for the past 15 or more years. He recently earned his 7th Dan black and I remain forever humbled at what he has become. I don't stay I touch with you like I should, brother, but you are in my heart always.

As I mentioned earlier, the Kobura Dojo that I founded so many years ago has continued its course and at one point I am told we surpassed producing over one hundred black belt practitioners. We pray that every one of these practitioners we release into the wild will stay pure and true in their teachings and the Art will live on as it has for almost a hundred years. Bob told me recently student enrolment has been down but as a school we never really had or wanted a lot of students anyway, just enough. What we looked for were good students that would one day become good teachers and keep the art as pure and untarnished as Shihan Kori and Shimekake Sensei intended it to be. He says enrolments are down because all the kids these days want to do MMA. It's the lure of being a cage fighter because that's all you see on the idiot box anymore. When was the last time you saw a Judo or karate tournament on TV? See what I mean?

This is interesting to me because Shimekake sensei used to complain about baseball and basketball in Japan the same way. The younger generations were more interested in those things than their martial arts culture. For hundreds of years in Japanese schools the arts of Kendo and Judo were taught as a main part and staple of the curriculum. Now this is no longer the case and it is the feeling of my generation and older that these arts are soon destined to be lost or bastardized into unrecognition. All the older and pure decedents of these arts are dying off one by one. Shimekake saw this and put in me and a few others as seed to keep these arts as they were, and remain robust and alive.

In the USA, for example, a student is encouraged to reach always for that next belt level. Their ambition is not guided by the art, but the pursuit of the color and the position it holds over others. Shihan Kori said very little to me in the short time I knew him but I remember this. "Gaining a martial skill is never measured or rewarded. It is tested in combat and comes down to can or cannot." I believe this in my heart and will always. It has been demonstrated to me over and over in my walk through life, not only in the martial arts realm but in the realm of day to day life as well.

At a tournament many years ago there was this young man who could not have been more than 22-23 years old, a black belt with 5 gold rings around the tail of the belt, indicating he was a 5th Dan or degree black belt. It has taken me almost 40 years to get to 7th Dan, so this kid must have had x-ray vision and was able to leap buildings in a single bound. He was doing all this flashy kicking and jumping shit while he was warming up and strutted around like he was the baddest guy in the room. So his turn to fight rolls around and he steps into the ring and nails his opponent, a little white guy, in the head right away and scores a point. You can tell this guy now thinks he is something to behold. This is the part I like, so pay attention. He faces off again and this time tries some flashy jumping shit. His opponent takes one small step to the left and punches him square in the nuts. The guy hits the floor and turns green, little white dude hits him in the forehead and bounces his head off the floor like a basketball, the fight is over, little white dude wins. So what's my point? Well, that is my point. You aren't something just because you wear the tag; you have to earn it and pay the price of admission. Just as an FYI, the little white dude had been studying non-stop for 5 years and just received his Black belt the week before the tournament. How do I know this? Well, maybe I know the guy . . . . maybe . . . . just a little.

NOT A KID ANYMORE

What does it take to grow up? How do you know you are growing up? Is it some magical moment or dream with harps and shit playing in the background and a bright light that shows you the path? Is it an event? A sign? A near-death experience? Maybe it's the guys off Duck Dynasty going "Happy, happy, happy." Who the hell knows. The fact of the matter is that at any given young age you really don't know if your ass is shot, fucked, snake bit or powder burnt. I've been here over 50 years and I can no more answer this question than I could light a fart at 10 yards. My thinking is, there isn't one real or right answer and if anyone tells you about a moment when they grew up, call bullshit. The reality of gaining maturity is from an unending series of emotional, physical and spiritual things, times and events that educate you in life on a daily basis. These mold you to think and act certain ways in certain situations that are socially acceptable, or not. Some do it better and worse than others but no more wrong than any other. Psycho—and sociopaths are not included in this conversation, as they're in category all their own.

We have certain rules in society we are supposed to follow to be "PC" that people like me could care less about. I go my own way, take responsibility for my actions and ask forgiveness from none. I have lived by three simple words: Honor, Courage, Integrity. These are the things that have allowed me to grow up. Well, that and getting my ass whipped regularly helped some too, I'm sure. I guess what I'm trying to get at here is that at some point, I was no longer a teenager anymore but a grown man with responsibilities. I can't tell you the exact moment this occurred; no one can. I just know that it did. To show for it, I have the love of three beautiful children and wife, my health, friends who would take a bullet for me and a decent living. Can anyone ask for or expect more than that?

I am not a conformist and just about anyone that knows me will tell you right off, "That boy just plain don't give a shit. He will do what he thinks is right and not give one good God damn what you think about him or the way he is." That would be a true and accurate statement, folks, good or bad, even a little arrogant maybe. I trust myself only in most things; that way if things go wrong I have only myself to blame and myself to make it right. Leaving home forced me to look at things differently, like, for example, who's buying groceries? Where am I sleeping if I don't have the rent? Damn, I need to do laundry soon 'cause even the dog won't come near me and so on. Hard questions to any man or woman at any age on his own, but doable. I didn't always make the right decisions and it cost me more than I cared to pay sometimes, but I could always look in the mirror and say I did what I thought was right and rolled with it. The problem comes when you do the wrong thing over and over. What is to follow here are a few events in my young adult hood that kept me somewhat on the right road. The ages 17 through about 22 contained some hardcore lessons for me. Things happened that made me change lanes and directions several times, often the hard way, but change I did and made my way to this point for the most part only slightly brain damaged.

I lived in this small town when I was around 20 or so and shared this house with four others about my age. There were two other single guys and this couple and we all had our own little apartments. I never was clear what the couple did for a living but it soon became very crystal clear. I noticed things about them but never paid any mind and kept to myself. Things like they always seemed to have money but never went anywhere to work, or they seemed to come and go at very odd hours and there were always different people coming in and out of their place. Hindsight is the great teacher and had I been able to put all this together, I might have saved myself some grief, but that was not to be.

All was well in the Land of Oz for about six months until one Sunday morning when I was yanked out of my little world by a cop, handcuffed and read my rights. They went through my place and turned it upside down but would not tell me what they were looking for. Come to find out, everyone else in the house was in the same boat and the only ones who did not have that WTF look on their face was the couple. I didn't smoke dope or drink then, as I was doing my best to get on the Olympic team and that too would change in the later years but again, another story. So anyway, the cops finally tell me they are looking for dope and that this house is known for selling dope. I immediately pipe up with, "Not me officer." He apparently didn't give a shit and off to jail I went, again. Christ on the cross, this was getting old.

Come to find out this couple were doing some big business out of our humble abode. The couple named everyone in the house as accessories, stating we knew what they were doing and even sent them customers. What a pile of shit. I couldn't afford an attorney so I took the jailhouse attorney, who couldn't have given a shit whether I lived or died and consequently, I took a little heat for his lack of defense. The fact was, I knew nothing of any of it, and I think the judge saw that in me and knew I was telling the truth and that I didn't have a dog in this hunt. He called me a victim of circumstance because the facts were I knew these people, we had some common friends that I had introduced to them (not to buy dope but apparently some had) and I lived in the house. The two other guys got off their charges because they were innocent and had real lawyers that actually gave a shit. I was the only one the judge gave an option to. He said I could go to basic training in the Army and have no criminal record or do the equivalent probation and public service but would have misdemeanor a record. The Army thing was a new program that had been started to deter would-be lifelong criminals. I was none of the above but I believe the judge had my best interests in mind giving me this option. If I completed basic and stayed out of trouble all was forgiven but if I got in any more trouble, the Army would have me for two years. Either way I would not have a criminal record, so off to be a soldier I went.

Basic was 11 weeks and was harder than I thought and I just made it harder because I felt I shouldn't have been there in the first place and stayed pissed about it for a while. My attitude adjustment came in the form of running around the parade ground in the rain with a rifle over my head, cleaning floors with a 4x4 inch piece of rag and doing pushups till hell started freezing over. I was in good shape already but this was a different kind of shape. This worked your mind and your body. The guys you see on movies and commercials yelling and cussing you, they are real and they are really in your face from sun up to sun down. They are not there to hurt you, but to break you down then rebuild you the Army way. The Army doesn't want you to be a robot but they do want everyone to talk the same language and focus on the same goals; to accomplish this everyone is trained the same way. What you don't see on these movies and stuff is that these drill instructors just want the best for you. They want you to be strong enough to survive on your own in any situation, but especially in combat.

I behaved myself, did my stint and left it behind. I had the option to stay and they asked me to, but I had other plans, namely the Olympics. I had no idea that years down the road I would revisit this option and this time I wanted to be there. The epilog to this story is that the couple that started all this bullshit ended up getting in more trouble later on and the guy was killed in prison. I'd like to say that's too bad but I'd be lying; sorry, but I just don't have anything for that one.

Not too long after all this Army shit we found out the Olympics was not going to happen, so now what? I didn't wander the streets crying, sleeping in dumpsters and drinking ripple wine or anything, but I know now that I was under some form of depression. I was pissed cause I had poured my life into getting on the team and felt it had been taken from me and I got fucked over without so much as a reach around. Here is where I lose my way for the first of two times in my life. I want to make it clear up front that I am not in any way justifying my lapse to the dark side and by this I mean I went into self-destruct mode.

I got involved with some people who were, for lack of a better term, pot heads, with no real ambition, goals or desires other than to smoke dope and show up at the next party. Of course I didn't see them that way then; to me they were the shit and I was having a hoot smoking dope and partying every chance I got. I had moved into this apartment building and this is how I came to meet some of them; the others I met on the job I worked at bouncing in a night club. As per the norm for me, there was a girl in the mix and I was thinking with my little head instead of the one with the brain in it. (The having a brain part has been under debate several times also.) I should have figured out that being a bouncer wasn't an occupation to be enrolled in just by the amount of physical damage I took from fights I was involved in at the place. As usual, though, I didn't figure it and one night it almost got me killed.

There is nothing worse or more aggravating than dealing with a drunk. Even now as a cop I don't do well with these assholes, but I have just learned handle them differently because you can never tell how they will react. They can go from nice and cooperative to a total dangerous dickhead in a blink. The place I bounced at was huge, with five different clubs in the place, and on any given Friday and Saturday night there would be upwards of 1500-2000 people spread throughout. This called for a lot of staff, being very alert and on top of your game. The SOP (standard operating procedure) was always to get a situation, whatever it might be, under control quickly, quietly and get it outside.

One night I get a call from one of the bars: "Get there yesterday because there's a knife fight going on." I show up and it's not really a fight but one guy who's really shitfaced threatening another guy with a knife. It wasn't any little pocket piece either; you could have hacked your way through the Amazon with this thing. I walk up and start talking to knife guy, trying to get him calmed down. I am standing between him and the guy he's threatening, about two feet from the knife. Things are going well and I am 95% sure I have this ole boy talked into putting it down and leaving quietly when some major fucking asshole decides to be a hero and jumps him from behind. Knife guy falls forward and guess where the knife ends up, my fellow homo sapiens? Yep . . . right in the ole chest, about 4 inches above my heart. Strangely, I didn't feel shit at first, I guess cause I was busy trying to get knife boy separated from Captain America on the floor. My first realization was when the knife got bumped in the scuffle and I see blood dripping on the floor, combined with the pain that damn near made me pass out. I am looking at this thing sticking out of me but other than it really starting to hurt, I feel fine. Nonetheless, it's a sobering moment seeing a six inch blade sticking out of your chest. As I said, I got very lucky with this one because an inch to the left and I would not be sitting here telling y'all about it.

The partying shit started gradually and just escalated from there, after work, weekend parties, Martin Luther King day, Lincoln's birthday, Passover, etc. I never did any hard drugs, **ever**, just the weed and that was more than enough and often too much. My booze of choice was Tequila with the standard lime and salt combo. I could have put this on my Cheerios. I liked it that much. I never tried it, but you get the idea. Trying to get women to let you lick the salt off of their various body surfaces was also entertaining and a highly obnoxious practice on my part. Sometimes it worked, though; it depended on how shitfaced they were. The problem was I liked tequila but tequila didn't like me. Some of the worst hangovers ever were on this shit but, I found that if I tempered the tequila with a joint or two or three I didn't feel like warm dog shit the next day. This was real science, folks, worked out all on my own with multiple field trials and experiments. I'm pretty sure it's not Nobel prize type of science but the data was pretty solid.

Ever notice how you have no problem doing shit drunk that you would never even entertain doing sober? Sometimes I wonder if the world wouldn't be a happier and more pleasant place to be if we all walked around with a buzz on. It probably wouldn't work out well for us if like NASA engineers, nuclear scientists, surgeons, school bus drivers and other high tech jobs were pot heads, but just a thought. Sorry, again I have digressed.

Anyway, it was nothing for me to smoke a joint at least once a day and more on the weekends. It got where I would miss it if I went a day or so without one. Not like withdrawals miss it, just that warm fuzzy I don't give a shit feeling you got with it. Tequila was different 'cause I could take it or leave it and most of the time I took it. I looked forward to the weekends 'cause there seemed there was always a party to go to and if not, you created one of your own and stayed fucked up the whole time. At times, going to work on Monday after one of these weekend benders was some kinda rough brother but I never missed work or got shitfaced at work; after all a guy's gotta have rules, right? It never caused me to lose a job either . . . well . . . there was that time I hit my boss in the mouth and called him an asshole. Don't act so surprised, I told you I wasn't too bright. Anyway, he asked for it.

So here is the tequila story I promised you earlier. I love ZZ Top and found out they had a concert coming, so of course there was no question I was going. So I saved up some vacation time and scored the tickets to a concert that was in a large city a short drive away. Road trip! We all loaded up on a Saturday, making sure there was plenty of booze and dope. There were six of us that started the trip, and this is important information to have later on, so pay attention. We get there; I am already wasted. Like the worst wasted I have ever been in my life. I will apologize right now, folks, because there seems to be a rather large gap in my memory on this trip and therefore in the story. All I can really tell you is that I regained some semblance of cognition two days later at some girl's house I had apparently hooked up with 250 miles from the previous concert city. Remember the six I started out with? Well, now there were only three, including me, and I didn't recognize any of these motherfuckers. Not only that, I had purchased, somewhere along the line, tickets to the ZZ Top concert that night. No recollection, zip, nada, nothing. Did I go to the concert? You're damn Skippy I did, no fear. Over the years I have had some flashes of memory of those few lost days but nothing I can really explain or weave into any kind of time line.

Life rolled on this way for a while until it started to really wear me down. The human body is not designed to be abused in this manner indefinitely, so I finally woke up and decided to get my shit together. I thought that maybe a change of venue was in order so I took a job in the North West Territories working for this airline company as a ground handler. You know, the guys you see at the airport running around the plane doing shit with the luggage and freight? That was me.

Now people, I'm from the South, where if it's below 50 degrees it is considered cold and below 30 degrees, we stock up on supplies to usher in the next ice age and throw another dog on the bed for warmth. I have lived in snow before but I have never, never lived in the cold we are talking about in this part of the world. There ain't enough dogs for this kinda cold and I'm pretty sure this is the reason they call it a wilderness. No one wants to live in that shit! Winter up there runs from about September through May and the average daily temperature is way below zero. Like I'm talking 20-40 below zero for months on end, and when there is a storm or a wind, the temperature falls even farther. One week up there we had a storm for about 4 days and the temp got to around 80 below that came with a frostbite warning of about 3 minutes. That is how long it took for your dick to freeze and fall off if you were stupid enough to unzip for a leak outside. You don't do squat in this kind of environment except watch stuff freeze. No planes in or out, nothing goes anywhere; even polar bears park it till it warms up.

From about November through March it was dark 24/7. I mean like the inside of your asshole dark. There was no daytime at all. Because of this phenomenon the airline made it mandatory that you had to go South for at least a week every six weeks because of something called "cabin fever". Ya . . . that shit is very real and I have witnessed it firsthand. People who are afflicted will literally go frigging postal, I mean way off the reservation. They start being paranoid, talking to people that aren't there, shouting at nobody, dressing weird and violent mood swings.

There were six of us that worked for the airline and we had rented this house that the airline leased. One guy that lived there wasn't the most stable individual you ever met to start with. He was just kind of an odd guy who kept to himself and smoked a lot of dope. He seemed to be very intelligent but also seemed to be overly concerned with the government and its shortcomings. Nice guy but personally, I thought he was already crazier than a run over dog. Anyway, he hadn't been South in about 4 months. He said he needed to save money for something and didn't need to go South; he was fine, but we had noticed some weird stuff had started showing up in his behavior. He would be up pacing at night instead of sleeping or we'd be watching TV and could hear him having a very animated conversation with someone that continued if he came out to the kitchen and so on. At some point he quit taking a bath or doing laundry because he started to odoriferously offend even the dog. He left his door ajar one day and one of the guys called me to see it because he had written bible quotes all over one wall with cartoon drawings to go with. The final straw was when Darrel woke up one night to find him standing over him in his room reciting something out of the Bible, he thought, over and over and would not respond at all. We got him to the hospital and never saw him again. We don't know if he went to a nut house to get plugged into the wall socket for a while or sent home; the company wouldn't say. We were asked to just pack up all his shit and put it on a plane.

Being in the dark all the time messes with your head, I can tell you. It was so cold and dark all the time and never any different. I had times there where I would just feel closed in, and it was very creepy. The opposite was true for the summer, because it was daylight all the time. You could go outside at midnight and it looked like noon, which was great for partying, camping and outdoor stuff but it messed with your sleep patterns a lot, so everyone put tin foil on the windows to get their days and nights in order. There was always things going on like 2 am concerts or 5k runs in the middle of the night just because they could. I was transferred to Inuvik for a short period of time because they were shorthanded at that base and this place is in the middle of absolutely nothing except some of the most beautiful scenery you will ever lay your eyes on. It was a lot farther north, cold as fuck most of the time and not too far from the pole as the crow flies. We had special suits we wore outside with heaters in them to ward off the cold because brother, it was a constant battle with you and elements. It was here I met Nate, or Nathanial to his family or if you just wanted to piss him off.

Nate was a full-blooded Inuit Eskimo, born and raised in Inuvik. He was also the only bush pilot around for miles, and I do mean miles—hundreds of them. I met him in a bar or "the bar", as it was called in town under some very odd circumstances. There are people out there who are just racist through and through and you can't do anything with them; they will not change and in my opinion, they just need killing. Even way up there was no different. There were some guys that worked on a pipeline and rig up that were in town and looking for some trouble and decided that Nate was a good target. I didn't know Nate at this time but that was soon to change. If there is one thing I cannot and will not put up with, it is a bully and if you're a racist bully you're even one step down from there. These two assholes decided it was pick on Nate night but no matter how this played out, I was on the Eskimo's side.

These two dickheads decided to get pissy and run their mouths because Nate was taking too long with his game of pool and they wanted the table. They began with the names and race comments and moved down to threats and cussing him out. I'm listening to this whole thing and watching Nate because two on one ain't a fair deal and I'm all about the fair deal when it comes to scrapping. To his credit, Nate said and did nothing until the bigger guy got up, grabbed the pool cue and shoved him. As usual with bullies, when they do their thing they have to have an audience and someone smaller to pick on, so I love this next part. I'm thinking Nate's gonna open a can of whoop ass on this boy, right? Nope, Nate doesn't do anything to the guy who just shoved him; he goes up and over the pool table, grabs one of the balls on the way, and hammers the other guy right in the head. The guy never had a chance and he hits the floor like a sack of taters. By now I'm on the move because I want a piece of this other guy before he can reach Nate. I jump on him from behind and do my best to choke him out but it ain't happening and it ended up looking more like a bronco ride at the rodeo. Next thing I see is Nate wind up like he's kicking for the Alabama Crimson Tide and drives this guy right in the nuts. Nate must have got him between the uprights because he goes down and the fight is essentially over. I got to hand it to Nate, he's not even breathing hard, grinning like he just won the lottery, and took both guys out with little effort on his part. The two assholes are escorted out by the constable, and Nate and I get down to doing some serious drinking.

Nate invites me for a ride in his plane, a Piper Cub a few days later, and I loved it. He taught me how to fly and I worked for him in return for lessons on my days off. His little plane was a hoss and we went everywhere in it. These Piper Cubs were designed like the Willie's Jeep, to go anywhere any time, easy to fix and easy to fly. I have over 200 hours in one these and in some of the worst weather conditions and places to land in the world, day or night. Very rarely did we land on ground, almost always it was snow and ice. Nate would hand me the controls when we got in some rough situations so I would learn how to get out of it and would wait till the last second to take over if

I wasn't doing so well. It scared the shit out of me but I learned. This guy could fly that Cub in and out of a duck's ass and not touch the sides; he was that good. He was also a good father and mentor to his two boys Charlie and Kandu (Native name after his grandfather). His wife Melisa could cook the shit out any part of the caribou you cared to eat and I loved his family like they were my own and was proud to show it. Because of him, I got my pilot's license when I got back to the world and kept it up for a while but opportunities to fly aren't abundant for a bush pilot, unless you want to shell out a few hundred dollars an hour to rent time. Nate was killed several years later flying a pregnant woman to a hospital and something went wrong on the landing. The good news is the mom had some minor injuries but she and the baby did fine. Well done, my friend, may God bless you and your family always.

It was while I ventured in the great white North I thought maybe I'd try and be a rock star. As you might have already imagined, there ain't a whole lot to do in the winter up here and so for entertainment we formed a little rock band. We weren't all that bad either, according to adoring fans. We weren't like a bag of cats anyway. I had learned to play the guitar when I was younger by teaching myself from the TV. On Saturday mornings there was this show called "Mr Guitar" and he would show you how to make chords and stuff on the guitar. So between that and a few song books I learned how to play. Now Jimmy Hendrix I ain't, but I got good enough to write a few tunes and play in a few bands. I even did some studio backup work some years later, as a singer not musician. Guess this is where my daughter gets her singing because I could carry a tune enough to be the vocals in a band, but I couldn't hold a candle to her. I did some solo guitar work in the graduate club at the university to make a few extra pesos while in medical school, so I didn't starve to death. The instrument I am most proficient at is the drums. I have been playing them since I was very little. Trouble with drums is you just can't carry those around with you real easy and it's hard to sing to just them, know what I mean?

Anyway I have gotten off track again. We were the "Northerners." Ya, I know, hindsight is always twenty-twenty and it's not the best choice of handles, but it did the job. We got a fair amount of work, especially in the winter. We weren't playing Madison Square Garden; however, it got to where we were playing almost every Friday and Saturday nights in places I wouldn't have let my dog stay in without his shots being up to date. But it was fun and most of the places gave us all the free beer we could pound down. Now imagine folks, if you will, a place that is dark, cold, with nothing else to do but fight, fuck and get liquored up. Some nights, I thought we were really just playing the sound track to some episode of "my big redneck family". Memories . . . God bless 'em!

So now what? I'd had about as much fun as I could stand up North and it was time to move on. Throughout all this, I had made my way back to martial arts pretty heavy and felt better physically. I had the chance to learn some other arts from guys I met up there and was intrigued with how they all fit together and with the spiritual discipline of these arts. I wasn't thinking about being a Buddhist monk or any shit like that; I just felt there was more to what I was learning and teaching. You know that feeling you have at times when you think something is missing or wrong? Like that. So as with most things I have set out to do, a few days later I am standing in downtown Tokyo. I literally decided on a Monday and was there on the Wednesday, an advantage of having no kids and spouse. I had no idea where I was going to stay, work or even how to speak the language, other than martial arts vocabulary. To be blunt, I didn't have a frigging clue. I was just hoping there were a lot of pictures to point at to get my point across and find my way around.

JAPAN

If I had ever had the chance to live in Japan for the rest of my days I would have; I love this country that much. I even tried to sit for their medical license boards but my language skills were not sufficient enough. I have traveled a good part of this globe and have never found the peace and attachment to any other place like I did this one. If you asked me why I couldn't even really tell you, I just do. It is a place like no other, rich in history, culture, scenery, people, customs and beauty. Mostly I think it had to do with the people. I was there for several years and the experiences I had there still influence me now in the way I approach life on a day to day basis.

I lived in one of the oldest areas of Tokyo, in what is called the Chiyoda prefecture. This is where the Imperial Palace is, among other things. The palace houses the emperor and his family, as it has for over a century, without burning down, as the previous ones have done for some 600 years. I taught English as a second language to the Japanese people and I worked for a school that basically set me up with the classes to teach. People of all ages took these classes. In true Japanese fashion, they did their best to overcome language as a barrier to business, to commerce and to perfect it as a social skill. At the time I was in Japan, the economy of the country was exploding. Japan was one of the few countries worldwide with a solid economy and also one of the largest exporters. You ever want to have some fun cuddled up to frustration try teaching English to someone who doesn't speak it, and when they do speak, they have an accent that makes it difficult to understand. I don't mean that in a mean way, I just mean try and teach someone like that what "dead as a door nail" means, or "y'all, I'm fixin' to" or "mad as a wet hen". Almost impossible, believe me. It usually ended up with me doing some kind of spur of the moment pantomime, cartoon drawing or charade show to get an idea across.

Chiyoda was also one the areas frequented and occupied by the Yakuza, or the Japanese mafia, as they are better known. Don't think of them like the Mafia of the USA lore and legend because there is a very gross difference and distinction. A short history is in order for y'all to understand what I'm talking about and how this relates later.

Despite uncertainty about the single origin of Yakuza organizations, most modern Yakuza derive from two classifications which emerged in the mid-Edo Period (1603-1868): *Tekiya* are those who primarily peddled illicit, stolen or shoddy goods and *Bakuto* are those who were involved in or participated in gambling. The Tekiya were considered one of the lowest social groups in Edo (the original name for what is now known as Tokyo). As they began to form organizations of their own, they took over some administrative duties relating to commerce, such as vender stall allocation and protection of their commercial activities. During Shinto festivals, these peddlers opened stalls and some members were hired to act as security. Each peddler paid rent in exchange for a stall assignment and protection during the fair. Because of the economic situation during the mid-period and the predominance of the merchant class, developing Yakuza groups were composed of misfits and delinquents that had joined or formed Yakuza groups to extort customers in local markets by selling fake or shoddy goods.

The Bakuto plied their trade in the towns and highways of feudal Japan, playing traditional games such as Hanafuda and dice. They were mostly social outcasts of various types, living outside the laws and norms of society. However, during the Tokugawa era, they were occasionally hired by local governments to gamble with laborers, winning back the workers' earnings in exchange for a percentage. Many of the Bakuto covered their bodies with elaborate tattoos, which were often displayed by the shirtless dealer of a card or dice game. This fashion led to the modern Yakuza's tradition of full-body tattooing. As the Bakuto organized into groups and expanded into other operations such as loan sharking, half of the groundwork for the modern Yakuza was born. (The other half came from the Tekiya.)

So now that you have an idea who I'm talking about, I will get on with why they became important in my life. At the train station near where I lived, built right into the stairs was a little noodle Kiosk run by Kenji and Keiko. At this time Kenji had to have been in his late sixties to mid-seventies, as was Keiko, and they had owned and run this kiosk for over 40 years. It was a local favorite and a well-known spot to those of us who lived there, including members of the Yakuza who also lived in that area. The long and short of it was I spent a great deal of time at this place and got to know these Yakuza guys known as *Kyodai* and *Shatei* (Big and Little Brothers). This has something to do with how they are organized, so if you want to know more, look it up. These guys are not as bad as they sound; at least, I never saw that in them. They were just regular guys that I did some serious drinking and partying with, during which, by default, I would learn how to speak Japanese and they English. It is amazing how easy it is to learn another language when you are shitfaced. I think it has to do with being more relaxed, with none of the usual inhibitions to slow you down. Because of my relationship with some of these guys I had the privilege of teaching English to their kids, wives and relatives. One of my classes every week for an hour had about 15 people of all ages in it from the neighborhood, a lot of fun and just great people.

At one juncture my Japan visa became invalid for some administrative reason and they were telling me that I would have to leave Japan and apply for a new one before I could come back. This could take several weeks to process and I had nowhere to go except back home. Over several shots of sake and beer one night I just mentioned this to one of my Yakuza buddies. A week later I received a message that I could come by and pick up my new visa. I could never prove it, nor did I bring it up, but I'm 99% positive those guys had something to do with it.

In Japan, even in the major cities like Tokyo, crime is almost non-existent. As an example, on several streets in neighborhoods are vending machines that dispense beer and alcohol. No shit, a vending machine. This thing turned itself off every night at 11pm and came back on at 8am for your drinking pleasure. Can you imagine machines like this in our cities? Shit, that thing wouldn't have been plugged in but a New York minute before it was in the back of someone's pickup truck on its way to a new home. In Japan, it was never touched other than for what it dispensed. In Shinjuku station, which is a main station hub in the train system, there is an area that is two floors underground and easily the size of a football field that has nothing in it but vending machines. You can buy anything from condoms to food, to suits complete with shoes (no shit—with shoes), flowers, jewelry, pet food, any magazine you can think of, toys, car parts, porn movies—you name it, it's probably in there. Y'all are probably thinking so what and I guess I don't blame you because this has to be seen to really appreciate it.

Over the course of the years I spent with the Japanese folks, along with martial arts interactions and teaching English, I became pretty fluent in Japanese and developed a deep love for them and their culture. You can't swing a cat in that country without hitting something or even someone that reflects their history, heritage and culture. In a lot of areas in older cities there are centuries-old buildings and temples still standing smack in the middle of a circle of modern skyscrapers—a weird but powerful image. Japan to me is one of those few places on earth that you never grow tired of and there is always something to see and do.

I am sure some of you have heard of a place in Tokyo called "The Ginza". I will not even begin to try and describe it to you, other than to say you have to see it to believe it. This is the Rodeo Drive of Tokyo and believed to be one of the most luxurious shopping areas in the world. This is where the rich bitches shop; there ain't no Walmart here. This is kind of strange because this area started out as a swamp that got filled in around the 16th century and was named after a Silver-coin mint that was established there. One of the things that it is famous for is the community of men and women that live there called "Geisha". I must apologize up front because this is where I take up my trusty sword and shield to become a defender of the faith (or the Geisha), so to speak.

Geisha have often been labeled and portrayed as a form of prostitute or high class hooker. This really came about during the occupation of

Japan after the Second World War, where common prostitutes called the cat house they worked in a "Geisha house." This also could not be further from the truth. Some true Geisha do perform sexually, but not in the sense you know of from seeing Miss Susie rotten crotch standing on the corner in downtown pump handle USA. These ladies (and men) are picked from very young ages, children, to be Geisha and are highly educated and highly trained. They typically can play several musical instruments, speak more than one language, sing, dance, paint, and are experts in all cultural ceremonies and traditions.

Geisha literally but roughly translates into English as "performing artist or artisan". Their origins begin around the 600s where, because of civil war, they were more the prostitutes we recognize now than the Geisha of today. In the 16th century and later, the Geisha became more refined and socially became more accepted as a very high standard of achievement and social status. Traditional Japan of this period embraced sexual delights of all varieties and the men were not constrained to be faithful to their wives. The ideal wife was a modest mother and manager of the home where, by Confucian custom, love had secondary importance. For sexual enjoyment and romantic attachment, men did not go to their wives, but to courtesans. For this reason, Geisha were also schooled in the art of giving sexual pleasure and technique, as this was often a requirement of the court and/or Royal house they lived in.

Thanks again to a few of my Yakuza friends, I have personally been to a Geisha house and seen their arts and performances first hand. To say it was beautiful is not to give it the justice it deserves. (No, I did not do anything my mama wouldn't approve of.) They are truly a Japanese treasure. If you ever want to see these ladies, they often can be found on the Ginza going about their daily list of things to do wearing the traditional Kimono and white painted face.

According to modern Japanese scholars, "The geisha remain one of Japan's most steadfast traditions and cultural deities that have remained almost undisturbed and unchanged over the centuries and a testament to the Geisha's true cultural beliefs and roots." I could be here all year talking about Japan but time is short, y'all have probably about had enough and I'm getting more wrinkled by the minute, so the last thing I wanted to touch on is the train system in Tokyo.

Now ladies and gents, I am going to do my best to convey to you just why you should have with you at all times a helmet, jock and mouth guard for this event. In my humble observation, this should be a spectator sport on ESPN or something just as worthy. Being in the big train stations at rush hour was the best, 'cause anywhere else in the world is going to charge you for this kind of entertainment.

Imagine if you will, several cylinders of aluminum on rails, each designed to hold, say, about 50 people the way it was built to do, now has 20-25 extra folks in it. The train would pull up to the station and the doors open; from here all bets are off. If you're on it trying to get off, you had better pray you were well positioned or you can hang it up. I don't mean just in the right place to get off, I mean head down and positioned similar to a linebacker. At the same time, those on the platform waiting patiently (in the same position) are pushing to get on in a human wave. Now the Japanese are sticklers for accuracy and being precise. This means the train is going to be on time both coming and going; you can literally set your watch by it. Sooo . . . to ensure this happens they employ these guys to stand at the back of the entering crowd and push like hell. Ya, just like that. They get bent at the knees, back against the throng and push like their life depended on it. It's amazing because it works. The people in the train car are squeezed into every nook and cranny until they can get the doors closed. Then it's off to the next stop and wash, rinse, repeat.

The truly amazing part to me is the Japanese people are so complacent about it. They couldn't give a shit because it's the norm to them. It is the way things are and have always been. This would never fly over here; we are too bitchy, arrogant and self important. How do you move 6 million people a day on a system designed for 4 million? Like this, that's how. It was a never-ending sense of humor and fun to head down to Shinjuku station at rush hour and watch this shit roll out.

My time in the land of the rising sun imposed changes and ideals on me that I carry and treasure even today. The education I received there was in my opinion better than Ivy League. As you are surely aware, things that affect you that deeply are for the most part, extremely personal and difficult to explain to others lacking the same love, detail and passion. On this you're just going to have to take my word for it. I encourage you to go there, see for yourself, and we can compare notes.

What I did have coming back was a great deal of issues with the English language and Western culture. It really was weird. I was so tuned into speaking and listening in Japanese every day in most everything I did that I rarely spoke English unless I was teaching it. When I got home I literally had to translate things into Japanese at times to grasp what was being said to me in English. My mom or friends would talk to me and I would answer in Japanese and have no idea I had. I even dreamed in Japanese. It was an adjustment in a daily routine, diet, sounds, cars, landscape and the very size of things in the USA. In Tokyo space is at a premium and there is a very large population, around 13 million at that point, consequently all the buildings are crammed right next to and often on top of each other. Nothing is wasted. You should see how they get their mail! That is a whole other story but a very interesting one. So coming back to the land of Nod where there is all kinds of space and not as many people was very weird and took getting used to.

Post the land of samurai and Toyotas, I actually started to grow up. No really, I did! Go figure, right? I went back to work as a carpenter and went back to school. I won't lie, I did have some relapses into the world of degradation and wanton disregard for personal health and hygiene but they were brief and far between. I even stayed in one place for longer than a year and with the same address. I did not have any run-ins with the PoPo, no fights or lapses in memory from one town to another, just a regular human existence. I spent a great deal of time teaching martial arts and trying to prepare solid instructors to maintain the Kobura School for the future. I guess I thought this was going to be my legacy or some soft-hearted sappy bullshit or another. The years following involved a great deal of change some due to mostly dumbass decisions on my part, failed marriages, career changes and the arrival of my children—none of which I regret, all of which I'd do again. Well, maybe not all . . . most, I think . . . ok, some . . . well, just the parts that didn't hurt.

MEDICAL SCHOOL

At one point in my quest to participate in the human race I was working as a carpenter. Not a very good one, but one nonetheless. I started out as a framer and moved on to finer things like renovations. I am nowhere near my son's caliber, that is for sure. I might qualify to carry his tools to and from the job site but that'd be about it. The guys who were my teachers in this craft were good and I learned a lot. We worked hard and drank harder most days. At one point as I crawled to work the umpteenth time with yet another hangover to listen to the saws and hammer go through my skull all day I asked myself, *Hey dick head! Is this what you want to do for the next 40 years?* The answer was very clear and I started looking for a change in career and drinking buddies.

Don't get me wrong, there was nothing wrong with this job. It just wasn't what I wanted to do until my hair and teeth fell out and I was back in diapers. The house I live in and the building I work in now were built on the backs of these people and without them we would be very, very fucked. My dad told me often when I was a kid, "The guy who picks up your trash every week is not to be pitied or looked down on because he does this job. You should be thankful he's there to do it for you." Without the guys who carry the bricks, dig the ditches, change your oil or stock the shelves in the grocery store, we would have some serious issues. These folks are the backbone that we call America. There I go again, going off on one of my rants—sorry. So I'm looking around and see this kid in the mall one day with a jacket on that had the name of some medical school on it and bingo! I knew what I needed to do.

Now folks, I reckon if you have never looked into going to med school and becoming a doctor before, it doesn't look like it would be all that difficult or complicated, right? That would be negative there, ghost rider. Holy shit, what a process. First of all, there are pre-requisites that are needed before you can even apply to schools and those better have 3.8 or higher GPA next to them or you can hang it up. I had part of a degree at this point and it contained none of the things I needed for medical school. You must have Organic and inorganic chemistry, Physics, English, Math and biology. They prefer you have a four-year degree before applying but it's not a must. These took me a little over two years to get done with night classes and trying to maintain my nutritional status with something more than Ramen noodles and rent via a job. Most days I would go to work about 0630, get off just in time to make it to class and eat supper out of the vending machine. Get home around 8 or 9 pm and have homework and studying to get done. Bed about 1am or so most nights, then do it all again the next day. Weekends were a bit easier as usually I didn't have to work so I could spend most of Saturday catching up on the Labs I had to have done by bright and early Monday. I don't think I got laid or went anywhere in that whole 2 year span.

So the next piece of the puzzle needed was the MCAT (Medical College Admissions Test). This is where a population roughly equal to that of a small country, all with the same desires, hopes, ambitions and motives, are put in this giant room for a fun-filled day of testing on all the shit you had just learned in the past two years. This test is supposed to weed out the useless and the frail by med school standards. I'm here to tell you, it don't. Useless was very prevalent in med school, trust me on this one. Once you have jumped this little hoop and you have MCAT scores, GPA, your application, three solid letters of recommendation (one from the pope, the president and Armed forces chief of staff will go along way) all put together with your essay on "Why you want to be doctor" and have sent them off to your choices of institution, the fun begins.

These chosen institutions are under no obligation to even look at your shit. I was once told to fuck off just based on my age. I wasn't the usual kid applying to med school; I was a tad older than the usual snot-nosed brat doing this dance. In my opinion, these kids who go from high school to college to medical school to residency never experience the world with the life and lessons it has to offer. I think that's why a lot of doctors are assholes, because they never learned how to be with people. In med school it's pounded into you that "You are a doctor and must act like one." Bullshit, it's my job, not who I am. It should be part of the entrance to med school that you have to have been out in world for 5 years before you can apply. Ya right, like that's gonna happen. The world is an unforgiving bitch and you learn in a hurry who and what your place is in it. I have a great distaste for anyone who acts like they are better than someone else. There is no such thing in my world and no one is better, just different. Doctors are one of the worst for this kind of attitude, followed closely by lawyers and corporate CEO types. Not all of them, but a good percentage. If you ever want to get a feel for Medical school mentality watch a Robin Williams movie called "Patch Adams". It is a true account of a rare individual and expresses my personal view of how a doctor should be. You'll enjoy it.

So anyway, now you wait to see if you're going to get the interview or the piss off letter. Even the interview is no guarantee of anything; they're just trying to put a personality to the face you sent them. This was probably the most aggravating part to me because there were no lines to follow or rules and it was totally subjective. Hell, they might not like the shirt you were wearing in your profile picture, maybe your ears stuck out too far—who knows? Regardless, you made your daily trek to the mail box everyday that summer waiting on your life to go left or right. I applied to 8 schools and got interviews to 3. I was at my final interview and already had been turned down by the other two for God knows what and I am sitting there with the clinical dean trying my best to not fart and present my best when she asks, "Why should we take you?" I sat there for a second and was about to give her a mouth full of the book answers when for some reason I got really pissed at the question. I don't know, maybe because my dick's bigger than yours or because if you don't take me I'm going to punch you in the uterus. I didn't say those things, of course; even a redneck has to set limits. What I did say was this: "Ma'am, I don't have a bullshit answer to give you that you haven't heard before or already anticipated. What I do have is a work ethic, along with a set of morals and values and expcriences that will make me a good doctor, and I will be a doctor whether you take me or I have to start over again." She didn't flinch, not a muscle, and I'm thinking, *Nice going numb nuts; you just blew that one. Why don't you go ahead and kill yourself immediately if not sooner.* Four weeks later I was accepted so I reckon she must have liked my honesty or just the fact no one had ever answered her that way, who knows. The next time I saw her was at graduation but for now another page had just been turned and I'm on my way to Medical school.

To give y'all an idea how my mind operates, just for shits and giggles I sat for the VCAT (Veterinary) exam and applied to some Vet schools just in case it all went to shit on the other end. This was my backup plan while I regrouped. Strangely, I scored higher on the VCAT than the MCAT exam. Go figure, and here is the really stupid part: I got accepted to a Vet school on the very same day my Med school acceptance came. Now what, right? My mom figured it for me and said, "Well, if you go to vet school you can't work on kids. But if you go to med school you can still work with animals" Thanks Ma, love you.

That August I'm on my way to the rest of my life. There were 205 in my class at kick-off, most of them nice people and some I remain close friends with even today. Others, on the other hand, were not so nice and needed killing right away. These are the ones who did whatever they could to suck up to professors and whoever else was needed to advance their career. These are the people that think nothing of throwing others under the bus or standing on their shoulders because it helps them get ahead. These kinds of animals just sicken me. Medical School is hard enough without having to deal with these assholes as well. But deal we did and in particular there was one guy who we called "the Nose" because this fucking thing got to the corner way ahead of the rest of him—I mean way ahead. Big ole honker you could park a frigging truck in. I really disliked this asshole from the minute I met him. You ever meet someone and right from the get-go there is something about them that sticks in your craw? This was him. So anyway, this little prick would do things like go to the library and take all the required reference books for the semester and hide them somewhere so he had them all to himself. How do you like that shit? Man, I'm pissed at him all over again and I could spend two pages telling you shit this dick pulled but I have other things to tell you at the moment. We did get to square his shit away before it was all over, though, in a way he will remember his whole life. I aint gonna give you details but let's just say it involved him being naked, molasses and bird seed and leave it at that.

First year was, as we say in the military, "a cluster fuck". It was all I could do to just keep my head above water. It was class, study, eat, sleep, exam, class, eat, shit, sleep, study and shit out what you had just studied; rinse and repeat. Every Friday was a test on some subject plus lab tests in anatomy, cell physiology and biochemistry. The way it worked was you spent all week studying for the next test, whatever that was, maybe anatomy, you take it, then start studying for the next one, maybe Bio chemistry, and so on it went with what we thought was no end in sight. There were six subjects in the year so by the time you tested for the last one you were six weeks behind the first one. It just sucked! Consequently, every Friday became designated as "Shitface Friday". You don't need to be a rocket scientist to figure what that meant. This form of academic abuse continued on into the second semester, where guess what, people? It just got worse.

This next part is just plain dumb on my part and I honestly wish someone had taken me aside and beat me senseless before I gave the nod to this one. The dean of education shows up one day to talk to us about those who might be interested in doing a master's degree in their second and third year med school. So guess who goes, "Yeaaah, great idea; let's do this, hooorah!" None other than captain dumbass himself folks. As if there wasn't enough on my plate, I asked for more and to make it worse, I was the only one who signed up. Now I'm committed to research, statistics evaluation and dissertation for the next two years. Dumbass.

Clinical rotations start in the third year and elective rotations in the fourth. This means you are out of the classroom and in the hospital. Now you'd think this is a good thing, right? Negative. It's an absolutely horrifying and belittling experience that borders on laws involving slavery and abuse. First off these folks—by that I mean the real doctors and nurses—just fucking hate medical students. We are stupid, slow, irritating, in the way and ask too many questions, most of them stupid. That's not everyone's feeling but at least half, I'm guessing. These dickheads seemed to have forgotten "from whence they came" and that they didn't wake one morning going "hey, I know all this shit!" Someone took the time and the patience to bring them along and get them where they are today.

Med students are cannon fodder and are inappropriately used in any number of different jobs and positions. For example, we can fetch things, take blame, do what others wouldn't and clean up others' messes. In surgery there is no one better than us to stand in some contortionist position absolutely still with our mouths shut, holding a retractor for hours on end. If you need someone to yell at and shit on because you just fucked something up, we are your man or woman.

Rotations are usually set up through Obstetrics, Pediatrics, Surgery, medicine, clinic and ER. You get several months in all of them, then you move on to the next. This was otherwise an uneventful year for me except for meeting Dr Obregon, or "Obeone" to a select few of us, who was the director of the ER in a hospital I was doing rotations at in Chicago and a very smart guy who loved students. He was a kind and gentle and above all a teacher. He had the kind of personality that made you really want to do well for him and you tried really hard not to fuck up. He treated you with respect and only asked you to be professional. "It's my job to teach you what to do, it's your job to do it as a professional" is what he would tell us. He treated us like we already knew what we were doing and that made us work hard to always be prepared. If he quizzed me on something and I didn't have all the info I should have, he would never say go and study this and then come back. He would say nothing and in that way said it all in a way that was inspiring rather than demeaning. I wanted to know it because that is what being professional is, correcting your deficiencies. I could guaran-damn—tee you I would know it back to front if it ever came up again. I learned a lot because he let me do a lot and most times he would go to bed and we would see the patient and call him with what we thought and wanted to do about it. His approach to me then is the same I use as a teacher today and it works. Thanks Obeone, you will never know how much of a positive influence you had on me and others. This is self evident, sir, by the lives I have been able to save because of your patience, knowledge and skill as a teacher.

Fourth year was something else all together. I won't bore you with the long details of what went on but I will impart one of those lessons we all seem to get when we really need it and we never forget it, no matter what. I was doing a sub internship, which means in a given rotation we function as the resident for that service. Mine was the ICU and I went in there like I owned the place and was about as cocky as I could get. This, I learned, is the wrong way to be because you can't learn in that frame of mind, and you tend to piss the nurses off real quick. An unspoken rule in any hospital is don't piss off the nurses 'cause they can be your best friends or the worst enemy. My attitude was reset to the factory requirements the first night shift I did and the nurses called me every 15 minutes for every kinda bullshit or another they could dream up. So and so's blood pressure is this, so and so's blood sugar is that, you need to come write the order 'cause I can't take it over the phone and so on, all night. They called me every 15 minutes about something trivial. By the time morning rolled around and I walked into the ICU dragging, beat, and tired, the charge nurse just looked at me and said, "Do we understand each other?" I said, "Yes ma'am we do." Lesson learned. From forth year it was on to residency.

I did my Residency in Pediatrics and it just sucked! Look up residency in the dictionary and it says: "To work your ass off for the chance to be abused and paid squat while doing it." It was a marathon in staying awake and being verbally and mentally abused by those who needed someone to beat up that day. Some parts were memorable but for the most part it was a blur of patients, conferences, tests, and whatever else came up that they could cram into your schedule. And you know what? I would gladly do it again 'cause in a sick kinda way, it was one of the best experiences of my life.

As a first-year intern it becomes apparent quite quickly that you don't know shit and need to carry the Library of Congress around in your pockets so you can answer the questions posed to you on rounds and noon conference. I weighed my lab coat one day and it was 24 lbs from the books, pens, assorted papers and the necessary tools of the trade you carried around to perform your craft. The other thing you need to have squared away as an intern is that you are everybody's whipping boy. If there is grunt work and low level shit to be done, you can bet your ass it will be on the interns' list of shit to do. It is a rite of passage almost as old as medicine itself.

The first night I was on call we had 18 admissions. I never saw bed till I got home that next afternoon. Here's how this would work. Say you're on call Monday. Then you are there all day doing regular patient stuff till 5pm, when the rest of the world goes home. They sign out all their patients to you with all the problems to be followed, labs to be looked at and notes to be written. In a hospital of 200 beds it can be a lot of patients. The on call team, which is comprised of typically 2-3 interns, a 2nd year and a third year with some struggling med students just for good measure, covered the PICU, NICU, ER, Floor, Cystic fibrosis floor, Heme/oncology, and the ICU step down unit. Usually you're up all night taking admissions or taking care of problems that come up. The next day starting at zero dark thirty is resident rounds, attending rounds, noon conference, notes, lab follow up and check out rounds. If you are lucky you can get out of there sometime mid-afternoon. You get home, shove some food in your pie hole and pass out. You're up at the crack the next day, which would be Wednesday and guess what? Your ass is on call again! And so the cycle continues all through first and second year. The only time I wasn't on call every other night was when I was on every night. The way I figure it, the residency program owes me about ten months of sleep. Yeah, like I'm ever going to see that.

I chose pediatrics because I absolutely adore kids and seem to relate well to them; it's their fucking parents I have issues with. God they can be stupid and retarded, not to mention, arrogant, neglectful, overbearing, self-righteous and self-important, violent, and just totally un-aware and un-caring. I say this because in my mind, parents can be the worst problems for their kids. They won't do what's told them because "they know their kid better than you do". Oh yeah, then why in the name of John Wayne's frigging saddle do you keep bringing them to me with the same problems? This does not apply to most parents, just definitely to a minority. There are parents that are blessed with disabled children and children with such horrible diseases you can't even begin to wonder where the strength comes from to get up every day to tend to these kids. These people have my deepest sympathies and greatest admiration.

The first time I ever saw a child die was in the ER as a student. It was without a lie, the most sickening and heartfelt thing I had ever been through. It took me weeks not to think about that baby, and I kept trying to understand what the parents were feeling and going through. I did not have kids of my own then so I had no real way of measuring it, and I don't know that there is a way of describing that kind of pain. The next child I saw die didn't bother me as much, but it still was difficult. Ladies and gents, I have pronounced more children over the years than I care to mention and I used to be able to tell you the name of every one. I stopped doing that some years ago for no other reason than the list just got too long and I came to understand these kids and their families are forever in my heart so I will remember them.

Residency finally came to a screeching halt and it was weird, really: one day you're a resident and everything you do is scrutinized by others so no mistakes are made because after all, you're a resident and therefore by default, retarded. The next day, literally, you're on your own, making your way through the medical world, praying you don't screw up and still carrying around the Library of Congress, only now it's on your office desk. I still have the handbooks I used in residency and I still use them every once in a while because you can't remember everything.

I finished on a Wednesday and the following Monday I am in my new office and practice, with only a minimal frigging clue what I was doing. My partner had been in practice a while so and his staff (I didn't have any of my own as yet) took me by the nose for a while, till I could get around on my own. We were the only pediatricians for 70 miles in any direction and they had a busy OB program and ER. We covered it all: floor, ICU, OB for C-sections, and the ER for trauma and admits. It was a lot like being back in residency but I was well trained—and that was tested on more than one occasion.

When you are standing in the OR at 2 in the morning looking at a 22 week gestation baby that weighs about a pound, things tend to get very real and you are up to bat until it's squared away. I have one of those personalities that in situations that are tense or under pressure, I am able to stay calm. I don't get rattled easy at all. This also was a blessing when it came to situations in military and police work. That's not to say I haven't ever been, it just takes a lot to get me there. I think one of the main reasons is because of Obeone. He would tell me over and over, "You can't think with your head up your ass, now can you?"

At some unknown point, I realized that working in a clinic is not what I was built to do. I guess it has to do with being ADD or some shit. I have to have more variety than just telling parents to stop feeding their fifty pound 3 year old Debbie cakes morning, noon and night and maybe, just maybe, he or she won't have diabetes and will be able to walk normally by the time they are in adolescence. I stayed in private practice for about 6 years and then folded my tent and moved to Mississippi for reasons I am about tell you in these next few chapters. By the time it was time to move I had gotten back into ER medicine and found that it suited me better, so I took a job doing just that and never looked back. I miss seeing kids every day but I am happy where I am right now.

FOR THE YOUNG'UNS

I have been everything from a guy who cleans toilets to the surgeon saving a life. I have delivered babies, cows, cats, horses and puppies and even piglets. I have been a policeman, soldier, doctor, personal trainer, teacher, carpenter, pilot, friend, brother, father, son and the Holy Ghost, amen. I have seen things I wish I hadn't and that no one ever should have to see. I've eaten things that would gag a goat and could not even begin to wonder what it was. I've had regrets that I've shouldered throughout my life that usually stemmed from my own stupidity. I know what it's like to be hungry, without a place to live and have only what was on my back. I have known love like no other and a disgust at some people and things that originated from somewhere deep within. Hate has always been a distant word to me, but I think if I could define it better I have probably come close at times. I have been in situations where I really thought I wasn't going see another day and others that gave my butthole such pucker you couldn't have pulled a pin out of it with a John Deer tractor. Of all that I have been and tried to be, the job that I covet the most is "Dad". That one I have earned the whole way and without a doubt, is the toughest job on earth.

When it comes down to it, I am a very simple man who does his best to live by simple ways and rules. Obviously I am not going to live forever, regardless of how many miles I run, hours in the gym, or eating healthy all the time (well, most of the time; I have a fetish for jelly beans). Along the way I have picked up a few things that have made sense, helped me to the next step or just sounded like something I should know, or do and pass on. What follows are just that, things I am passing on to you the reader and to my kids: use them, don't use them—whatever; they are there for your perusal.

Laugh a lot, it's still the best medicine.

When you argue with your significant other, hold their hand. It's really hard to argue that way.

If you want to live free of pain then think of others first.

Crunchy beats smooth peanut butter even on the worst of days.

Read everything; there is always something to learn.

Tell the truth even when it's not on your side. You won't regret it.

You are responsible in this life for your family, your health and your word. You lose sight of these and you have nothing.

Push yourself, be uncomfortable with it. That's where the growth comes from.

Be yourself no matter what others think you are.

Someone should always take up for the weak and the invalid when needed; let it be you.

Seek out mentors. They will guide you, challenge you and keep you between the ditches.

When you have a blister, put a big whack of Vaseline on it, put your sock and shoe back on and get back to it.

Friends are there always, no matter how bad, rough, dangerous, or sad. That's how you know they are friends.

Seek balance in your life. Have goals and pursuits but try not to accomplish them at the cost of your loved ones.

Discover what you're passionate about. This will give you focus in life.

Honor, Courage, Integrity. These are not a given. You need to earn these, and there is no higher accomplishment.

Treat everyone with kindness and respect until they give you reason not to.

Everything you do makes a difference. You just have to decide what kind of difference you want to make.

Recognize in others the difference in judgment, as opposed to errors in their character.

An error only becomes a mistake when you do nothing about it.

Drink from the garden hose.

Don't try to live above your raising.

Don't ever settle in love. It may take some trial and error, but that person who is for you is out there. They will be the one you can't be without because it hurts.

Faith is personal, no matter who or what you believe in. Allow others the same path.

You never get a second chance at a first impression.

Take time to listen to the world and allow the sun to warm you.

Family is everything.

Put mustard on bee stings.

There will be no greater love you will feel than the day your children are born and no greater fear than when they are hurt or missing.

If you want your shoes dry by morning then stuff them full of newspaper (no shit, it works).

The greatest smells in the world are babies, horses, fresh cut grass and puppy breath.

Every day learn something, help someone and try something new—now that's living.

Farts are always funny.

Ice to bruises and heat to muscle pulls.

Believe you can and you're halfway there.—T. Roosevelt.

There is no such thing as a stupid question.

Despite what is quoted, some things are solved by violence.

Righty tighty, lefty loosey. (Except on bicycle wheels . . . go figure.)

Face your fears. You rule them or they will rule you.

In the words of the great philosopher Forest Gump, "Stupid is as stupid does."

Manners are the difference between a gentleman, a lady and a hog.

Forgive, even when you don't want to.

Shit does not always roll downhill. At times it can and will go sideways.

Pay it forward.

There is no excuse for being filthy. Soap is everywhere.

If it walks like a duck and quacks like a duck, it's gonna be a damn duck.

Someone is going to break your heart, so get used to it.

Don't put the empty milk container back in the fridge. It pisses people off.

The greatest SEC team ever is the Tennessee Volunteers. (My book, my team)

If it smells, don't eat it. I don't care how fresh it is or who made it.

Friends are like peeing in your pants. Everyone can see it but only you can feel its warmth.

I know some of you are going, "What the hell is he talking about? I hate crunchy and I hate the smell of puppy breath." Well boys and girls, that's because it is life. We may have all got here the same way, but we are all different and that is the spice of life. If more people recognized this in the world we could spend more time helping instead of hurting or killing one another.

As I have stated earlier, this isn't the world I thought I would be leaving you kids. I'm scared, worried, disgusted, paranoid, and just plain don't like it. I will have no way of protecting you once I'm gone and that does not set well with me one little bit. For the longest time—years—I felt like there was no need to be this way. I thought that raising my kids right, with the right values and intentions, would be enough. It is not. At times I almost feel like they need to have SEAL training just to survive. For many years I never kept a gun in the house or even contemplated the idea. Now, I don't go anywhere without one.

So what changed? How did I get this way? I do not have an easy, straightforward answer, but basically I went to work, had interaction with the public, turned on the TV and watched the world around me turn into an ugly, scary place to be. It seemed almost overnight that the world and a good portion of the people in it went to the dark side. It's not all bad, I know, but what I have seen and have worked through far outweighs the good. Granted, in my careers as an ER doc and a policeman, I have definitely seen the worst humanity has to offer. Has this tainted me? You're damn Skippy and can't be helped in a lot of ways. When you're exposed constantly to something, you start to be that way and begin to believe it is the way things are. It's like eating in Waffle House: no matter where you sit, when you leave, you smell like Waffle House.

I don't apologize for passing on these paranoias because I want my family to always be prepared and vigilant. Is there going to be a zombie apocalypse? Doubtful, but notice I didn't say no way. I'm not a doomsday prepper in any sense of the word, because I think those folks are out of control. How retarded do you have to be to prepare to the extent these people do, then go on TV and show the world where you are and all your shit is? You really think the guy down the street from you who sees you on the TV, knows exactly where you are and what you have is preparing the same way? That somehow you've inspired him? Hell no. He's figuring on how to steal your shit when it all hits the fan. Zombies—no; mass destruction, famine, disease, civil unrest, economic collapse or world war? Absolutely—those are entirely feasible. You can't totally prepare for these kinds of downfalls and chaos; it's impossible but what is possible is to have your shit squared away, with your family educated with some simple plans and sound thinking.

As a cop, I have taught active shooters classes to the public in several instances. Those of you who don't know what active shooter means, allow me to briefly explain. It is a class taught to large groups of people, schools, colleges, hospitals and targeted businesses that teaches them what to do and how to react to a person or persons coming to their place taking hostages and/or shooting people. It is a difficult concept to get across because most people cannot fathom that kind of fear or have never been in anything like it, so their reactions are untested. It is the natural instinct of people to panic and be fearful when these situations are presented. My job is to teach them how to deal with these reactions and turn them into positive actions that may save their lives and those of others. I have taught my family in the same manner. The question I always wonder about during these sessions is why am I having to teach this at all.

In grade school I remember that once a month or so we all had to practice for the event of a nuclear bomb being dropped somewhere nearby. To survive a nuclear holocaust all we had to do was get under our desk—remember that shit?! They obviously have never seen the footage of a nuclear bomb and the destruction it can invoke. Under the desk ain't gonna cut it, boys and girls. The point I'm trying make is that we had to actually practice for that event for the same reason active shooter classes are taught, I'm guessing. People are out of control and don't give a shit for or about anyone or anything except themselves.

I don't remember my parents being paranoid about where I was or who I was with because for the most part in those days it was a given that you were safe and the world could neither get to you, nor hurt you. People cared for each other and took care of each other's families. I'm also not saying child abduction, murder and molestation never happened; I'm just saying not near to the degree we see it today. It was nothing to find 1 or 2 extra kids at the supper or lunch table on any given day at our house. There was an open door policy that as long as the opposite set of parents agreed and knew where you were, any and all were welcome. I never even heard of a predator or ever remember seeing the news about mothers killing their children by putting them in car and pushing it into a lake, someone going into a school and killing innocent kids, or drowning your kid and burying her then going out partying like a rock star every night. Not only that, the bitch got away with it!

I don't have any solutions to any of this or some fascinating words of wisdom that the Dalai Lama would be proud of. What I do have are some experiences, a lot of training and a can-do, will-do attitude when it comes to securing my family, the weak and the invalid against those who would hinder, disrupt, maim and hurt rather than help folks in their daily lives. It is the law of the wild that allows the weak to be dominated by the strong, but not while I can do something about it. Those people that care only for themselves will be self-evident when or if the situation ever warrants it, and you will have no problem spotting them—that I promise you. I'm not talking about the Alamo here but it is along those lines that I envision things as a future unless we can find our way back to a simpler time.

I'm going to preach a little to y'all but specifically to my kids a minute. Education—get some. Get all you can because it is the key that opens most doors now and in your future. If you had told my dumb ass that when I was a teenager I would have said yeah right, and walked away giving you the upright middle finger because I knew everything and that's all that was needed at the time. Gone are the days where you can make a decent living as a laborer, a waitress or store clerk and be happy with that as a means of getting by. It's different now; you have to have more and that more is higher education. I don't mean like I did, where after twelve years in school I finally got to work; I mean education that is going to get you a career and a way of life you can be happy with. I can't guide anyone on this except to say look around and ask yourself what is going to be needed in the future that I can prepare for now? That could be a direction to head out in but you have to follow your heart on this one. Whatever direction you decide to go, make sure you are doing it for you and not 'cause someone else is influencing you to. Strive always to be the best you can be. I asked my dad when I was kid, "What should I be when I grow up?" He said, "I want you to be more than I was, but above all, be what you want to be in your heart." Sounds legit to me.

Finally, I want to share a poem with y'all that I learned back in high school that has been an inspiration I have tried to include in my walk through the years. It's by Chief Tecumseh of the Shawnee Nation.

> *Live your life, that fear and death can never enter your heart. Trouble no one about their religion. Respect others in their view, and demand that they respect yours. Love your life, perfect your life, beautify all things in your life. Seek to make your life long and its purpose in the service of your people. Prepare a noble death song for the day when you go over the great divide. Always give a word or a sign of salute when meeting or passing a friend or even a stranger when in a lonely place. Show respect to all people and grovel to none.*

> *When you arise in the morning give thanks for the food and the joy of living. If you see no reason for giving thanks the fault lies only in yourself. Abuse no one and nothing, for abuse turns the wise ones into fools and robs the spirit of vision.*

When it comes your time to die, be not like those whose hearts are filled with the fear of death, so the when their time comes they weep 'and pray for a little more time to live their lives over again in a different way. Sing your death song and die like a hero going home.

POPS

In my alone moments as a kid I would wonder why my dad was such a mean and violent individual. What made him that way? None of my friends' dads were like that, at least from my perspective, anyway. They never came to school unable to sit down, not able to do gym class because their legs, back and ass hurt so bad from being beat with a web belt. They weren't walking around like they had a broom handle stuck up their ass. As I grew up this question changed in some respects but remained a bitter and unanswered thought for the most part. Some answers came later in the form of my grandfather and how he was to me and I'm sure to my dad growing up. I'm gonna get around to this sum-bitch here in just a little bit. The facts still remain: he was physically very hard on me and my siblings. An ass whooping was a big deal because you were going to hurt and he was over the top a lot of the time. Were there times that did I need a good ass whooping? Absolutely, but often not to the degree it came in. In my personal view, a lot of what is wrong with the generation today is they don't get their ass kicked enough, but the way I was done—no child should have to be abused like that. Don't get me wrong for a minute, I loved and respected my dad and even into my fifties I think of him and miss him daily. By the same token I do have issues with the way he brought me up and the way he handled discipline at times.

It never occurred to me till sitting down to write this that I know very little about my dad's childhood. I remember a lot of the things he told me about his childhood but it doesn't amount to a whole lot. Dad "Buck" as he was known to the rest of the world and "Pops" to me— was 5th generation military, born and raised in Toronto, Canada until joining the military in 1954. Apparently he was a pretty good hockey and baseball player, from what I was told, and he did a lot of sports growing up, so I guess that's where I got that tendency from. Being an athlete growing up you would have thought he would have known that smoking was not good for you. Nonetheless he and John Paul lit 'em up constantly. Secondhand smoke? Never heard of it, not in those days— why the hell I don't have lung cancer yet I just can't figure. When we were in the car or at home with Pops we were smoking right along with him the whole time. It was always better when it was warm out cause he would have the window open in the car. The rules on smoking were different then too, because it was actually advertised to be cool, trendy and socially acceptable to smoke. They even had advertisements showing doctors lighting them up.

I was named after my dad's best friend, who apparently died very young but from what I don't know, and neither did Mom. His mom's name was Katherine, Grandma "Kat" to me. Now here was an enigma I will never get. She was married to John Paul, my grandfather, one of the worst pricks on the planet, and she was the polar opposite: sweet, kind, resourceful, gentle and apparently also one of the few on the planet that had the bluff on John Paul. According to Mom, she could put him in his place with just a look and a few curt words. That right there is something I would have bought a ticket to see. Buck entered the Army as a 2nd lieutenant and made his way through the ranks to captain and through flight school as an Army helicopter pilot. This job took him a lot of places, including the military college in Kingston, Ontariom where he met and married my mom, Ellanor Ann—"Ella" to everyone else. They were then posted to Fort Rucker, Alabama where in short order, my ugly head came into the picture.

Pops had a temper on him and the problem with it was, it was just like John Paul's in that contained a physical component to it that was often to the excess. It was never just one swipe with the belt; it was 5, 10, 20, give or take, depending on how mad he was. This was followed later by a 2 hour sit down (after he calmed down) on why the world turned and the price of shit in China. I think this was his way of justifying the carnage he dished out and maybe there was also a tiny sliver of apology hidden in there for us to dig out, but he would never say it. Our legs, thighs and butts were so tore up most times that we often bled from some spots and were bruised and swollen so bad on others that walking was a problem. There definitely was no sitting for a few days, and walking looked like you had a stick up your ass. Once I managed to catch a lick in the nut sack 'cause I moved and instead of just being a few days' recovery, it was more like a few weeks. Sitting was definitely not an option. God help you if you put your hand in the way to fend off the blow 'cause that was going to take a lick to.

Mom could smack me all day long with whatever she could get in her hands and it never bothered me. I will give credit where it's due 'cause when it came to wielding the broom handle she was the best around. Grandma Kat would cut this thin, short switch and tear up my legs, and buddy, that shit hurt. She would stripe my legs from my ankles to my ass. With these two, though, it was absolute martial discipline and felt that way 'cause I got outta line and they put me back on it. John Paul would hit you in the face or the chest, usually the chest, with the back of his hand in a full wind-up and it would literally knock the breath out of you. One time I tried to dodge it and it caught me in the throat. I really thought I was going to die right then and there cause I felt like I couldn't breathe and he could have given a shit.

It was always the weird shit that ended up as a session in the punishment chamber. Case in point: we were in the camper visiting some friends of my parents when lo and behold, my mom's jade jewelry was nowhere to be found, so guess what? We were all guilty without trial and were sentenced to belt lashings from Dad until one of us admitted we had taken them. Really? What are an 8, 7 and 5 year old going to do with it? Fence it at the local pawn shop for lap dances? As I remember, it went on for quite a while then lo and behold, Mom finds the shit in her drawer, wrapped in some clothing. Go figure. So now you would think we might be due an apology or hey, sorry for the ass whooping and torture for the last few hours—my bad, let me make it up to you. No, we get this: "I'm sure one of you was messing with it and that's how it got wrapped up that way." Really, Dad? Really?

It was years later, long after Dad had been gone, that Mom confessed to me she thought Dad was way outta line that day and several others over the years. She told him so behind closed doors but it was already done and firmly embedded in our emotional careers. Of course, I had to ask

Mom why she didn't step up to the plate and tell him and maybe spare us a few layers of skin. She said she did not say anything at the time because that was the way things were done then. Things like this were discussed later, out of child earshot. If one parent disciplined the other backed their play, regardless of their belief in it. In a way I understand that now with my own kids, because if my ex-wife doesn't back me on my kid's screw-ups then it makes things a whole lot more difficult later on because now she thinks it's ok. There has to be a consistency.

The belt was one thing, but as I got older the methods changed. We went from little kid's rules to the big boy ring almost overnight, it seemed. Case in point: my dad could cuss like a sailor and often did around me but never around my mom 'cause that was a huge no-no. Unbeknownst to me at 12 years old, there were rules for me cussing around him also, and rule number one was don't cuss and smart off in the same sentence. I don't remember the exact way things went but it involved me saying, "Why the fuck should . . ." The last part never got out because I was unconscious at the time. We were in the garage and he hit me so hard I went over the hood of the car and woke up on the floor. That was the first time of several where I have no recollection of time for at least that moment. That was also the first time he had ever slugged me with a closed fist.

So why have I been whining about this for the past few pages? Because my Pops was huge, well over 6 foot, and all of 250 lbs. His fist was the biggest I have ever seen; even today it's still in the top ten. That thing had to be 8 inches across. At best, growing up I was 90-100lbs at 12 years old, so I am sure you get the picture and the fear factor here; he was a very intimidating man, even when he was not angry. He was one of these people you just didn't want to mess with. To put this in better perspective, whatever unit he ended up in with the Army, at times they had to build the cockpit of the helicopter so he would fit in it. Now that's a big dude. I don't think he would be that imposing to me now as an adult, but I never got the chance to find that out, either.

As I have already told you he was a chopper pilot for the Army and we lived in Lahr, Germany at the time. What I have not told y'all yet is the circumstances leading up to him getting killed. There was this huge earthquake in northern Italy with lots and lots of death, damage, destruction and people there were hurting in a big way so the unit my dad was in was called in to help. Before I go blithering on, let me back up for just a second and give you another piece that goes with this story.

I could never lie to my dad 'cause he was like some kind of master Pink Panther detective and could always tell when I was. I still gave it a shot a time or two, but for the most part I never did. About a week before all this Italy stuff came in to play, he had asked me to clean up the storage locker downstairs and I didn't do it. It was my habit to get up with him in the mornings, make his coffee and go out and start the car, especially in the winter time, so it would be warmed up. On the morning he left for Italy, he asked me if I had done what he asked and cleaned up the storage room. I boldly lied and said "Yes sir." He told me what he always did when he went away: "You're the man of the house while I'm gone; act like it." He kissed my mom and that was the last time I ever saw him again. I won't bullshit you on this, that moment was probably the worst regret of my life. I carry it with me even today and I feel just as ashamed. Strange to feel that way even this far out but, guilt is guilt I reckon. You know what the worst part is for me? The not knowing. I like to think he died not knowing I lied to him but I will never know. The night we got the news of him being killed one of the first things I did was clean the locker up. You could have eaten off the floor. It may have been therapy; it was shame definitely. It didn't take the pain away but it did give me a small measure of relief.

In short Dad was flying a rescue mission that went horribly wrong and it cost him everything. There was a wire where there shouldn't have been one and he hit it. The wire let go at its mooring and wrapped around the mast of the chopper (the part the blades are attached to), and they fell like a rock. According to the two people that survived the crash, if Dad had not done the things he did when they were crashing, they would not have survived either. As one of the survivors said, "I've never seen anything like what he did, then or since." That, my friends, is the ultimate eulogy for anyone. "Greater love hath no man than to give his own life for a friend or a stranger." Kudos, Pops.

My life at this point kinda took a nose dive. Some would maybe call it a teenager rebelling against authority; others might say he was expressing his inner anger at the loss of his father. Me, I call it being a dickhead to my Mom, plain and simple. At the ripe old age of 14, I knew everything. You couldn't tell or teach me shit and I was ready to take on whatever the world had to give me—or so I thought. What I had was a bad attitude and an even worse temper. I basically told my mom to kiss my ass, I'm outta here. I lied, pushed and cheated my way around to get what I wanted or what I believed was the way it should be, because no one else had a frigging clue except me. I hurt a lot of people and will never be able to take it back or make it right. The real problem was I didn't fear my mom, therefore I went off the reservation with no worry of corporal punishment or any other form, really.

Did my dad leave me with a giant hole? Indeed he did and still today I can't see across to the other side of it. What I realized too late was I used the energy of that trauma to do some pretty bad things instead of making things easier for my mom, who suddenly found herself in a foreign country, without the man she loved unconditionally, with three kids and the wonder and worry of how she was going to provide for them. Thank God for the military because they are their own family and world unto themselves, especially back then. My dad had a lot of friends, plus the people who worked with Dad stepped up and carried a great part of the load for us. To y'all who might be reading this and know who I'm talking about, my deepest and most heartfelt thanks. Even today that sounds so trivial compared to what y'all did for us. Thankfully, my dad had some things in motion in the event of something like this happening that came into play and really eased things for my mom.

So help me out here. How can you miss someone who beat you half to death most of your life? I don't know, just lucky I guess. Years later, when I thought I wanted to be a kick boxer (another dumbass idea) for a while, I got knocked out in the ring and taken to the local ER. They checked me out and took x-rays of my jaw and neck. The doc comes in and says, "Have you ever broken your jaw and neck before?" I gave him the affirmative on the jaw, compliments of my dad, but had no idea about the neck. So he proceeds to tell me that at some point in my life my C5 vertebrae had been broken and not really healed just right. I thought about this a while then I remembered.

Not too long before Dad died, I sassed my mom just a little too close to my dad's hearing radius, and this infraction of the law was a taboo above all others. He proceeded to beat the living hell out of me, and I mean closed fist and angry to the point my face very quickly became unrecognizable and I lost consciousness at some juncture in the event. For weeks after, my neck hurt like hell but it was only one of several pains I was dealing with at the time, including my jaw being broken, so I just thought I pulled something as my head was being taken off. What really was going on was my neck had been broken. I never saw a doctor—you just didn't do that back then unless you were dying—and it gradually got better and I went on my merry little way. Thanks Pops, appreciate it.

I'll tell you what really confuses me about Pops. He could have these episodes of such violence when he was angry or felt we had done wrong in some way, but I only ever once saw him demonstrate this in a public way. We were young; I think I was about 6 and we were playing outside at this hotel playground. There was this older kid—I say kid because he was at the playground too, but was much older than me and he was smoking. Anyway, he starts picking on me and hits me on the side of the head and of course, I'm not putting up with that bullshit so the fight is on. My little sister goes running to my parents' room to tell whoever would listen and my dad comes flying out just in time to see this guy hit me again. He reached me and this guy in about 3 strides and smacks this kid in the back of the head. Holy shit! I'm thinking, *This youngster is about to die.* The kid gets up and runs to a room on the end and the next thing I know there are two older, bigger guys coming out of the room, yelling some shit and heading straight for us. So what does Dad do? He practically runs at them, cold cocks the bigger asshole and knocks him the fuck out right there. I would swear that ole boy was out in midair. The other fella beats a hasty retreat and the cops show up. I don't know what happened at that point but we all went to Dairy Queen after they left, like it never happened. It was never brought up or ever spoken about, ever.

I want to tell y'all my favorite Pops story, then we will move on to other mundane things. My dad didn't have a racist bone in his body but what he did have was zero patience for those who were. He and Mom were posted to a base in Georgia when he was a young lieutenant and at this time of course, the bases, like a lot of other places, were still segregated. So when my parents arrive there they are told that they will have to temporarily live on or near the black area of the housing on the base. Apparently it was put to them in a more descriptive manner by Dad's commanding officer but I won't repeat it verbatim here. This, of course, was fine with them but his commanding officer told him that he should not be seen fraternizing with black people while in uniform. That pissed Pops off big time, so what does he do? He has a BBQ at his house and invites all the black officers he can find—and his commanding officer. As you can imagine, it went over like a turd in a swimming pool but he made his point and there wasn't a damn thing anyone could do about it.

On the total opposite of the spectrum of Pops was the officer and the gentleman: the military side of him that demanded perfection, manners and 110% effort in whatever task was undertaken. On the base there was what's called the Officers Mess, a place where officers went to relax and have drink or just to meet socially and formally. There was also one for the enlisted soldiers for the same reasons. My pops felt that we needed to be schooled in how to act proper at the mess and to be schooled on formal etiquette while at the table and so on. At our house my mom didn't lift, carry or open shit on her own; we had better have it done for her or we answered for it. As an example, one time we were going into the house and I wasn't minding what I was supposed to and my dad saw Mom open the door herself instead of me. Well holy shit, you would have thought I stabbed her for all the hell I caught, but that's how it was in our house—no exceptions. Anyway, Pops went on this crusade of sitting us down at a table and teaching us how to eat at a formal table setting, where the napkin goes, how to eat a chicken breast with a knife and fork, how to pour wine and a ton of other shit that at the time I felt was as useful as pissing into a hurricane. It wasn't until years later I was very grateful for that training when I really needed it.

I never got the chance to get big enough or skilled enough to open a can of whoop ass on my dad. I'm not saying that like it was a lifelong ambition or anything, I just wanted a little payback—retribution, if you will. I wanted to knock him around some and make him hurt a little, as he did me. These, of course, were adolescent and immature thoughts but came from a place within me that felt it was justified in some way. If it had ever happened the way I fantasized, I think he would have woken up with a different point of view and a little more respect for me. I loved him all the same, no matter what I have bitched and whined about here. Think what you will about my pops but he would be the first to stand up and take his licks or admit he was wrong if he was. Not only that, he would go to great lengths to make it right, no matter what it cost him. Thankfully that little quirk was passed on to me and I am proud to own it. There are several things I don't and won't pass on from my dad. The most serious of these to me is I don't dish out corporal punishment to my kids in anger. If they need a spanking I cool off before it is given and that is to their benefit as well as my sanity. A few times, though, I have broken that rule and paid for it with guilt, embarrassment and a quest to make it right with my soul. There have been other lessons learned but I'm not going to bore you with them except to say I believe they have made me a better dad. Isn't that really the definition of being a parent—the lessons learned? Pops would tell me over and over growing up, "All you're born with is your health, your word, and your family; you fuck those up and you have nothing." I can't tell you the number of times I have repeated that to my kids. Maybe they will listen to the old man while I'm still here to see it. God, I hope so.

MA

I saved writing this chapter till almost last 'cause I needed to make sure I had it right and I didn't leave anything important out. "Ma" is what I have called my mom for as long as I can remember and boys and girls, this lady is my hero. She is the person I aspire to be like and the single one person in the world I have infinite respect for. I hold black belt ranks in six different martial arts, I'm a soldier and a cop, and I will never be as tough or as stout as this woman, ever. By the time I get done telling you about her, I hope you will feel the same, or at least know where I'm coming from.

She was the second youngest of six children born in Manchester, England and had it rough right out of the shoot. The family was poor as dirt and being a young girl during WWII made things that much harder. Her family scraped by with the minimum every day, just trying to survive economic depression and war with a single mom trying to provide and care for them. Ma and her siblings would go out early most mornings to follow the coal truck around the neighborhood and pick up the pieces that fell off the truck because they could not afford to buy it. Y'all are sitting there right now going why the hell would they be following a coal truck? Well, at that time, coal was the main source of heat in most homes and coal mines were a major source of employment in England, even today. Most houses had a fireplace that burned coal, not wood, and in all the back yards there was a coal bin they stored it in. Mom's father left them for another younger woman when she was young and never supported them one damn bit with anything. The way Ma explained it was he walked away and couldn't have given a shit. Ma saw him one time some years after he left and apparently he acted like he could have cared less what happened to any of them. What kind of man can walk away from his kids? I never met him, thank goodness.

Mom shared her bed and her clothes with all the other kids in the house. ALL of them. Clothes were passed around between each of the boys and girls till they were worn out or didn't fit anyone anymore. Ma would often have to wear her brothers' clothes because they were all that fit her. Food was at a premium, in part because of the war, but mostly because they couldn't afford a lot. Her mom worked morning and night at two jobs and the kids took care of each other. Nothing went to waste. You know the fat that congeals in the frying pan after you cook a hamburger? They used to save that in a tin can and spread it on a piece of bread for their supper. How does that sound for y'all's next meal? They tried not to miss school because they would give them snacks and milk during the day and that is about the only time they would get milk. You never saw a doctor if you were sick; you gave it your best shot at the house. Even if a doctor was available to see them they could not afford the medicines.

She had an older brother, Patrick, who went to war, landing the day after D-day, and was killed by a sniper and a younger brother that died at two years old from pneumonia. Her one older sister, Elsie, was in my opinion a bitch. She was just one of those people I was never comfortable around, and she had one son, David, who was one of the biggest douche bags I have ever known. I never liked the little prick nor he me, which suited me just fine. Within a day of our first meeting David and I were trying to kick each other's ass and throughout our childhood it stayed that way. To give you an idea what kind of asshole he was, after his mom passed he let my mom know that he wanted nothing to do with her. No explanation and no reason. The thing about all this is that his dad, Uncle Stan, was a great guy and I loved him to death. He was always smiling, nice and pleasant to be around and doing his best to be a good dad and person. Him I miss; his son I could care less about. Shit, I have gotten off topic again. Sorry.

As I said it was war time and because Manchester was a major industrial city the Krauts targeted it for bombing a lot, almost nightly, and you may be familiar with this as the Blitzkrieg. Because of this bombing campaign, a good number of the children were fostered out to families in the surrounding countryside and smaller towns that were safer. Enter Vinnie and Jack Castle. They took my mom in as a war orphan and cared for her like their own. I never had the honor of meeting Jack; he died from the Asian Flu epidemic that ravaged the country in the late forties. I did, however, have the distinct honor and pleasure of knowing Vinnie as I grew up, and she was an amazing lady. Four foot high and four foot across the beam, with held more laughter and love than two people. She was the matriarch of the family and everyone loved Aunt Vinnie. Vinnie was there when we got the news about Dad and was a tremendous support to Ma, despite her own pain and advanced age.

Ma stayed with Jack and Vinnie about 3 years, till the end of the war, and then went back to her mom and sort of finished school by the British standards of that time. It would have been about the equivalent of grade nine to us but don't think for a second she was anything but literate. That woman can work a crossword puzzle like no one I have ever seen. I will admit, her handwriting takes some work to figure, but then so does mine and half the damn world's. She left school because she had to go to work to help support the family, becoming a seamstress and a pretty good one, too. She made a lot of our clothes growing up and we were lucky to have them. Her mom died when she was 22 and so she and Elsie moved into this boarding house together and continued to work. Get this, she would make 22 Shillings a week working daylight to dark. A week, not a day! This was the equivalent of about $2.50 in our money. How far you think that would go now? Can you even buy anything with that??

In 1956 Ma got on the boat to Canada. There was supposed to be Ma and four of her friends going to Canada at the same time, but for one reason or another they all backed out except her. A pretty gutsy thing for a young woman alone to do, I reckon. When I asked her why she chose Canada all she said was, "Because your dad was there." She landed in Kingston, Ontario and set up house in a room at the YWCA. A year or so into her journey, the YWCA had a little dance party and they invited all the officers from the local military college to it. Enter Ronald George, "Buck", a meager 1st lieutenant at the college and the rest, as they say, is history.

There are always things you remember when you're older that as kid didn't really strike you as odd or different or as something you should have paid closer attention to. Allow me to give you an example. We didn't have a lot growing up, but what we had came the hard way and we learned to take care of it. As a child I had no idea how my mom had grown up but I do remember standing in Kmart with my mom trying to buy a pair of pants for me for school, with me copping a really fucking shitty attitude because they weren't the ones I wanted. Normal kid shit, right, copping an attitude? Well, here is the rest of it: I also remember feeling embarrassed because my mom was wearing a pair of shoes with a hole in the toe and an old pair of pants that had been repaired God knew how many times. Did I put two and two together and think, "Hey! Shit for brains! She is wearing clothes and shoes that are worn out so you can stand there in Kmart with a shitty fucking attitude because you don't like the BRAND NEW PANTS she is buying for YOU!" No, I did not make that connection then but as I got older I did see it, and a lot more. I cannot begin to guess at the sacrifices this lady endured for me and my siblings and in years later, when I asked her about this she said, "Boy, I was raised with nothing so I was already used to it. I took a step up from where I was when I married your father." When Dad went it became even harder for her and true to form, I thought of my own self first and neglected the one person I should have been there for. I have already proclaimed what an asshole I was and I have done my best to make up for what I could. If Ma asked me right now to move a mountain three feet to the left, all I would say is, "Yes ma'am, where should I start digging?"

Don't misunderstand me, when I was a kid and even up to a few years ago my mom was/is the fastest on earth when it comes wielding a broom handle. She could tear our ass up faster than a goose shits with that thing. As we got bigger Ma learned that cuffing us with her hand didn't do shit but annoy her, because usually all we would do is start laughing. So she fixed that issue and brought out the heavy artillery in the form of the broom and other assorted kitchen and household appliances. This, for the most part, got our attention.

As I have mentioned my dad ran a tight ship when it came to my mom. She was to be spoken to and treated as a lady, regardless, no exceptions, and failure to comply with this rule meant your ass. So being the little shits that we were, Mom covered for us a lot when we got outta line or did something wrong. It wasn't until years later that she told me that the reason she did that was because, "Your father would have taken it too far" and she was right.

He loved my mom like no other and she him the same way. You could see it between them when they were together. As a snot-nosed little kid or self-indulgent teenager, you don't recognize these things till later on and start to put it all together. When Dad died Mom was only 44 and a very pretty lady. She was asked out on dates several times on different occasions but never went. Whenever I have asked her why she didn't at least go on some dates she would always give me the same answer: "Because I love your father." She is at the time of this writing into her eighties and just as sharp as she has always been. She spends her time with her cat, watching sports on the TV, fussing around her house and whatever else is on her routine for that day. My sister lives about 2 streets over, so she is well looked after and wants for nothing.

Hindsight is always 20/20, I reckon, and I am not the only asshole who wishes he hadn't been one, I'm sure. Pops liked to tell me, "An error only becomes a mistake when you do nothing about it." This is so very true. I never understood just what was taken from her that day and what she had done with the strength and tenacity of two men to keep us and the family whole. I can only hope to become half the person she has always been and for my kids to love and respect me as much as I do her. Love you, Ma.

John Paul

This is going to be a short chapter because this prick just ain't worth the paper. I'm only including him because he played some part in raising me and I wanted to give you an idea why I disliked the bastard so much. I say dislike because I don't have another word to use at the moment. If that changes I'll let you know; meantime let's get this done 'cause I'm getting pissed just thinking about having to do this.

I really don't know a whole lot about this guy other than he was an asshole who lived with us for a while as he got older and we saw on and off as a child. He was from Toronto but was born full-blooded Irish, which is probably where the tempers in our family come from. He was ex-military, 30 years in service as a sergeant, but never fought in the world wars and I have no idea what he did. He probably made a career out of making other soldiers hate him, also. I guess these were all the questions I was going to ask my dad at some point and never got the chance and likely the same reason I don't know a lot of details about Dad, I guess. I think these are grown-up questions and conversations I would have had with my Pops had he been around for it. As a kid you don't give much of a shit about your grandfather's background, especially when you can't stand the bastard and give even less of a shit today. I spent as much time as I could trying not to be around him, which is about polar opposite to most kids and their grandfathers. I'd see him coming and get the other way like my ass was on fire and my hair was catching.

I learned very early that he did not care much for my brother and me. He would do things like go to the store, for example, and bring my sister a treat and not us, and although I never knew for sure, it seemed to me that he liked Steven the least. He would act different around my parents, but when we stayed with him alone it was a whole different matter. My first real recollection of how fucking crazy this prick was, was when my brother spilled bath water over the side of the tub and he got mad and held his head under the water. I was yelling at him to stop and that got me backhanded across the chest. We couldn't have been more than 4 and 5. Who the fuck does this to a kid? Of course we never said anything because we were afraid of him so nothing ever came of these events. At about 7 years old he caught my brother and me with a cigarette in the back yard. So instead of telling us it was bad and wrong, this guy says to me, "You're the oldest and should know better, so the punishment is on you" as he proceeds to put the cigarette out behind my right ear. Really! So if Steve shits his pants in front of me and I don't stop it, it's my fault for that, too? What about Apollo 13 getting fucked up in space? Do I need to 'fess up to that also 'cause geez, something that big should at least get my dick slammed in the door, shouldn't it? It's great logic if you are in the Gestapo but I didn't get it then and still don't get it now. There was no rhyme or reason to how he was to Steve and me; he would be nice as he could be then the next minute he's burning my hand with a cigarette for not closing the car door or some bullshit like that.

On Sundays after church he sometimes would take us for ice cream. I think he only took me and Steve because others were around. One Sunday we are walking through the drug store to the soda fountain (that's how it was then) and a young guy coming the other way bumps into me—no big deal, right?. Well apparently John Paul thought otherwise. He stops this kid and tells him he needs to apologize. Now I don't recall what the kid said but the next thing I know the kid is laid out on the store floor like fresh road kill. JP turns around and just walks off with us in tow, like nothing had happened, and left the kid laying there and never once looked back. To me he was the ultimate enigma because you never knew what he was going to do or say given any situation. Case in point: my brother slopped water over the edge of the sink onto the floor so what does JP do? He holds Steve's hands under the hot water. I rest my case.

After Grandma Kat passed he came to live with us until a few years before he got the fuck off the planet. He seemed to have changed as he got older. He was still a prick but calmer. He spent his days smoking, drinking, and playing cribbage with anyone who could stand him long enough. I remember my mom telling me that he was well liked at the bars and pubs he frequented; guess they didn't know him the way we did. My brother is a lot like that. He is the life of the party but in reality about as useful as teats on a boar hog.

Having just re-read this little chapter I realized I haven't said anything positive about him so here goes. I always liked the smell of his cologne and when I was a kid he gave me the rules for an argument I still use today when needed. The "three F's" according to John Paul, fit any situation or argument: "fuck this, fuck that and fuck you."

JP died alone, I believe a miserable old man. I remember my dad getting the phone call that day, standing in the kitchen, and he seemed to me not to care, almost relieved—or maybe he was just being tough in front of us. I don't know. Talking to my mom years later about him and his relationship with my pops, I got the feeling he wasn't missed by too many people, especially my dad. My mom, being the kind of person she is, would not come right out and tell me her true feelings but I got the idea. That's another conversation Pops and I never had. If there is a heaven or a hell, I hope I get to the one he's at 'cause I have a few things I need to tell him and with any luck I will get to punch him in the nose.

BROTHER STEVE

What a dick! That pretty much says all I wanted to on that subject.

EARL

Earl is my heart, as are all my kids, but she was the youngest and I guess I doted over her more than the others. Yeah, I said she 'cause her real name is Ronni Gen but I have called her Earl since she was very small. I think it came from one of the movies she watched all the time, "Earnest goes to camp". There was a character in it called Earl that she would mimic and so it just stuck. She wears it proudly unless there is a boy around she wants to impress, then it's "Daaaaad don't call me that." She was named after her grandfather Ronald George which, as you probably already figured, is where the Ronni comes from. The "Gen" is a Japanese word meaning summer, as she was born in June and fits her grandfather's initials. I wanted to call her George but her mom wouldn't go for it.

At the time of this writing she has just broken into the realm of a teenager, complete with all the hormonal, moody, selfish and self-conscious attitude that comes with it. As any parent will gladly testify to, brother, there is a lot of it. She is the youngest of three, having an older step-brother by 19 years and an older sister by 13 years. I tried to have a kid about every decade, that way I would already have a babysitter for the next one in line. Dysfunctional thinking maybe, but it's solid in practice.

I am proud to tell you that I delivered Ronni, born on time by elective C-section. As corny as it sounds I was in love with her from the very minute I got her out. As I was reaching in to get her she grabbed my baby finger and hung on like she knew who I was. I won't lie, I cried like a 3 year old because she was just so amazing to me. I had no idea at that point things were going to go the way they went or be the way they are today. I'm not saying I would have changed anything 'cause that would mean I wouldn't have Earl, but I might have gone about trying to raise her a little better than with the conflicts of divorced parents who don't always agree. Oh well, I do the best I know how and hindsight is always 20/20, right? Why do people like me say things like "hindsight is 20/20"? It's kind of like saying, "Hey dumbass, you should have probably known better and seen it coming." Just thinking out loud, y'all.

I met her mom during residency and apparently I had no idea what the fuck I was doing, really, but you make choices based on your best impression at the time. We separated when Ronni was two and it has been a battle ever since, on how Ronni should be raised. I suppose neither could be called wrong, just different. If you hear something often enough you don't question the validity of it unless something shows itself in direct conflict to that belief. As Ronni has grown, she has made up her own mind on what is true and what is not, and I'm sure at times lies in conflict as to what is right and wrong and what to believe and what not to from both camps. Don't get me wrong, she is a great kid. She has smarts, the tenacity of a pit bull, can sing, writes her own songs and is funny as hell most of the time, but unfortunately she is also blessed with my temper and her mom's mouth. This has a tendency to make her life less than agreeable at times and when it does, boy, is it on.

Of course the judge gave Ronni to her mom as the primary residence because I had a shitty judge and an even worse lawyer. I asked the judge flat out, "Why can't I be the primary parent? I can give just as good care as she can, probably better." The answer: "We always give to the mom, usually." "Why?" I asked. He says, "It's just the way it's done most of the time." Judge, you're an asshole. The end result was equal custody and I got to have her half the time till she started school. My friends, this was one of the most painful things I have ever been through. Handing your daughter back after having her for two weeks is very hard and made worse when the kid is crying for you and you can't do anything about it. I have been shot, stabbed, run over, beat up and have broken almost every bone in my body, and I would do it all again rather than go through that once.

Her mom took her back to Mississippi where she's from so it was almost 3 hours to meet halfway to exchange the kid 'cause I'm living in Alabama. That gets old too, and it's really hard on the child so eventually this called for a drastic solution. I packed up my shit, closed my practice and moved my happy ass to Mississippi. I told you I wasn't too bright, but I did it so I could be closer to Earl. It's what fathers do, right? It was still almost an hour and twenty minutes from where I moved to meeting her mom halfway but for several reasons there was no way I was going to live within arm's distance of her. It was hard to make that decision, but over the years I think it has proven to be the right one for the most part, other than I wish I could be more accessible to Ronni, especially now she is older and has all these activities she is engaged in.

Ronni had it a little tough as a kid. To date she has been in hospital several times for one reason or another, including some surgeries. She had bad tonsils so they took them out. She had a kidney stone when she was 10. Where that came from I don't know, because neither family has them. The last surgery really pissed me off but in a way is my own fault for not being closer so I could have intervened.

She was with her grandmother and was doing something she shouldn't and fell through a plate glass floor. Yeah, I said floor. I still haven't figured that one out, but anyway she got a couple of nasty lacerations to her face and arm that needed some work done to them. Thankfully that's all there was and it was not worse. She gets to the ER at a major trauma hospital for children and they decide she needs to go to surgery to repair these. Now I'm scared, right, because I have not seen these lacerations and I am going with what I'm being told on the phone. When I finally get a look at the damage, neither needed surgery; they were minor and easily fixed. I repair those all day every day in my job, but her mother insisted on the surgeon doing it. Not only could I have taken care of this in about 30 minutes, it was the worst sewing job I have ever seen from a surgeon. A monkey humping a football could have done better, so now when Ronni gets through with adolescence we are looking at some plastic surgery to remove the scar on her face. Why some people have to make shit out of sugar on even the simplest of things despite their best intentions I don't get. If it quacks it's a frigging duck, not a moose.

I think Earl worries herself into thinking there is an issue at times when there really isn't. She comes by it naturally because her mom's the same way. For example, one day I made mention to Ronni and her mom (I really don't have a lot of sense at times) that Ronni was very flat-footed. Well holy shit! Since then it has been orthopedists, physical therapy, braces and special inserts for her shoes and so on. Don't get me wrong, if she needs anything she is going to get it; I just think it gets focused on more than it should. I believe her mom has all the best intentions when it comes to Ronni and medical issues but it's over the top sometimes. I have no doubt that her feet do bother her, but it was never mentioned till I brought it up and even now she never wears the inserts for her shoes she's supposed to wear to correct the problem. One time, Ronni had several days with a headache and her mom was thinking brain tumor because she works with those kids every day. I think you get my point and like I said, it's not a moose.

Earl is a pretty cool kid. She has her quirks like we all do, but she doesn't let them get in her way most of the time. When they do, she doesn't always deal with them like I think she should and has a tendency to be too hard on herself and difficult with those around her, namely her parents, mostly her mom. A lot of it is just mouthy teenage stuff and will change with age I know, but it can wear on you at times. She is a teenager right now and into the narcissistic era of her growth. You know, where it's all about her and how she looks, especially to any boy who wanders up and also the group of "best friends" she has for this week. I love to hear about what goes on at school because you can't pay for that kind of entertainment with its never-ending series of teenage drama. I don't remember my friends and me being like that but I suppose we were. I believe it's programmed into teenager DNA that at a certain age you become this whole other person for a few years. This other person has no memory for anything except social activities and this includes but is not limited to keeping up with personal hygiene, and they have this language that is all their own. I don't know, maybe it's just me. What do y'all think—am I close?

She has talents others could only wish for. She is very funny, with a twisted sense of humor that she gets from me. Hell, I'd laugh at a funeral if it was funny enough, and she would too. Sing! Lord, that child can sing. She has this very cool sound to her voice, kind of a mixture of Kim Carnes, Melisa Etheridge, and Adele, and I love to listen to her. The first time I knew about this talent was her mom sent me a 2 minute a capella recording of her singing an Adele song. She was only 10 at the time and I had no idea it was her at first—it was that good, I shit you not. I was so amazed that I played it for some musician friends of mine and they too were blown away. This past year we got her into voice lessons and this has just made good even better. The school has students learning all kinds of instruments and others taking voice lessons, so what they do is every year they build a band comprised of these students and go around to benefits and perform publicly. Ronni has really taken to this being on stage and surprisingly is really very good for her age and experience. Do I sound like the proud papa?

She has decided all of a sudden to take up guitar lessons as well. Her mom tried to get her to learn and I tried to teach her on several occasions prior, but I'm just her dad, what do I know? The cute little eighteen year old boy that's teaching her knows a lot more and that's the way it is, Dad, so suck it up. Why is it when you tell or suggest something to your teenager they look at you like you have a third eye but when anyone else (preferably a cute boy or girl) says the same thing, it suddenly becomes a holy shit great idea that they have never heard before?

She takes after me in martial arts. She is into boxing and Karate that she learns from this guy, Larry, down the road from her out of his garage. She really likes Larry and I like the way he teaches. He and I are very old school martial artists with old school values and ways and he does a great job of imparting these to the kids he teaches. She seems to derive great pleasure in beating all the boys in the class and I think that's just being female, but she loves it. She will get on the phone excitedly telling me play by play how she beat some boy's ass at class. It's good to have goals, so I just hope she stays with it. Ronni gets easily frustrated with herself when things don't come as easy as she thinks they should and has zero patience; it has to be instant or not at all. She will grow out of this because her dad was the same in a lot of ways. Even now I get mad as hell if I don't get or understand something I feel should be a no-brainer.

She did the whole cheerleader thing for a few years in junior high but last year was the first time she had to try out and it didn't happen for her. She was pissed but surprisingly, she took it very well, better than I thought she would. She was more upset that a friend of hers got in and she didn't 'cause according to Ronni, "She can't cheer worth a squat." I don't know where she is on this right now but I will support her no matter what if she wants to try out again next year. To give you an idea of her personality, here is a little insight I got from her at age eleven. She came to me one day and said, "Daddy, I think I want to be a Marine sniper." (I have no idea where that came from.) I looked at her for a moment and said, "Ok, but baby, but you know Marines don't allow women in combat." She looked at the ground for a minute and then said, "That's ok, Dad, I will just stay here and shoot terrorists." Love that! A girl after her daddy's heart, and she was serious, folks.

When things come up she is the first in the center of the ring and a natural leader, the same as her dad. This isn't the best avenue of approach at times, but it is the way she was raised and the way she chooses to be. She will take up for the underdog every time and back her plays with heart. When she was 10 she called me one day, mad as hell at something that had occurred on the bus ride from school. Basically this older kid was picking on and slapping a younger kid and wouldn't stop. Earl took it upon herself to fix the problem by smacking "the asshole" (her words) right in the mouth with the warning, "If you want some more, then let's dance." I couldn't help but be proud of her. I don't encourage fighting for any reason, but in this case she was right and I cannot fault her for doing what I would have done. There is no fear in that kid most of the time, except when it comes to the dark—she doesn't like that at all. Despite what we are taught as children and by the church, some things are solved by violence.

Ronni has the same issues with school as I did when I was her age: basically I just didn't want to be there. Earl is very smart; she just doesn't want to be there either, but what kid is real happy about it? I know most kids are this way to a certain point but Ronni just plain couldn't give a shit. I know she can do the stuff; hell, she scored one of the highest on her SATs and was pissed 'cause she had to sit there and do them. She was in a private Christian school up to grade 8 and I was never a big fan of this school to start with because it was very narrow-minded and biased in its teaching. They would conveniently leave things out of history because they were not attached to some Christian value or any other reason they could find to sensor it. As an example, the slaughtering of the Jews by the Nazi in World War Two was not taught or mentioned because it was not a Christian value. There were other examples, but y'all get the idea. I don't know the whole reasoning behind Ronni changing, but she moved to the public school in grade eight. I was all right with that 'cause that's how I rolled in school but her mom wasn't quite so pleased about it at first. Some months later, I think Ronni wasn't sure if she made the right choice either, but she has stuck with it.

We are from the South and to be honest, the race issues of old are still very much alive in both camps, white and black, just quieter than they were in the days of Medgar Evers and MLK and in my opinion, we have not learned a damn thing. I think this was a factor in not wanting Ronni to go to public school in some people's minds. One of Ronni's first boyfriends was a mixed boy and there were problems with that at home, with her friends and so on, but she handled it just way I think she should have, head-on and on her terms. It's a pity our kids still have to grow up with that in their lives, but you just can't take a two hundred years of ingrained narrow prejudice, passed on generation to generation, and expect it to just disappear. I have done my best to raise my kids to make up their own minds on this, the reason being is that these are very personal and morally complicated issues that are a very large part of our moral character. I think what bothers her about this is that race issues are in direct contradiction of her Christian values. Earl seems to be very squared away on the race issue and has made up her mind that there isn't one, and that to me is good. How she handles the rest of the world on these issues is yet to be seen.

When I was going through the police academy, Earl was there as often as she could be or on the phone asking what happened in class. When we were learning stop and approach techniques she was right there, being a bad guy and a juvenile delinquent. She doesn't want to be a cop, she says, and I am glad of that. I'm not sure I could handle her being in harm's way all the time. However, if it's what she wants I will help her get there. Her mom won't like it but oh well, her mom doesn't want her to be in the military, either. The reason I'm bringing this up is when I got on the SWAT team she started training with us. She would get in the stack and clear a room just the same as we did, and she also knows a lot about Active shooter, how and what techniques and procedures are applied and when. So much so that she was quite upset at the policy her school had for this (virtually none) and told the principal so. She offered to have her daddy come in and teach the staff about it but they weren't interested in what she had to say. They said God would take care of them if something were to go wrong, and you can imagine how this went over with her. Ronni has her faith, but she is also well versed in the reality of the world for her age. She always says to me, "Daddy, aren't you glad you didn't have a girly girl?" No punkin, I'm just thankful to have you healthy and happy.

I have not always been the best father I could have, I'm sure. What parent is? Raising kids doesn't come with a manual and for the most part, it's a day to day hit and miss that you get right at least most of the time. We mostly base it on the rules our parents pushed on us that we swore we would never inflict upon our offspring. Yeah right, how'd that work out for you? When she reached her teens Earl had some mouth and temper issues and still does, most of it normal for her age. However, this kid could go from the tooth fairy to the exorcist in a blink. At times, she and I have had our not so pleasant moments and I end up putting another check mark in my "way to go, asshole" column. It seems this past year with her has been difficult and very hard on us. We always had a lot of laughs and good times but we seem to butt heads more these days instead. My wife tells me it is a phase that she is going through and all will be well in time. God I hope so, because nothing hurts worse than being in conflict with your children.

As of late, she and I have talked a lot about going in the military and she usually brings this up on her own, including asking about going to West Point Military academy. I told her she can do whatever she wants; the sky's the limit. I know she's young and has yet to have her heart broken by a boy, but it's coming and I feel sorry for him 'cause he's gonna get hurt. My point is she will likely change her mind several times on just about everything and that is par for growing up. I just want her to be happy with what she decides and know what she chooses is something she wants, not what someone wants for her. For now, it's the daily "ok, what's next?" scenario and my job description is still to protect her, advise her, run interference when necessary, maximize her options and most of all, love her always for the unique and beautiful person she is.

RARA

This one is my middle daughter, not by blood but every bit a huge part of my heart. Nora was a DHS (Dept. of Human Service) kid that frequented my clinic in Alabama, and she was 10 when I first met her and her sister Donnie. Talk about a shitty childhood. At the time we met, I think that was Nora's 8th foster home. Not because she was a bad kid but because her twin sister was not exactly normal and you could see that just by looking at her. It was never diagnosed until I saw her in my clinic that she had a condition called Noonan's Syndrome. Basically, it's very much like Downs Syndrome with some different features. Anyway, there were some behavior issues involved with Donnie and so they got moved a lot because no one wanted to deal with her. I say twin but they were but about as different as could be and they looked nothing alike and of course didn't behave the same.

Nora had 4 other brothers and sisters—same mom but with different sperm donors. Notice I didn't say dad or father because that would have implied participation in the children's lives, which didn't happen. All the kids were taken from the mom and placed in foster care for one reason or another, none of them good. I got to know Nora pretty good through the clinic and she came to the house a few times to spend some weekends with us. The ex-wife and I were still married at this point and Ronni had not as yet made her way here. The long and short of it was we decided that we would adopt her, so at 11 years old we had a daughter and I felt very lucky and privileged to have her. It was a little strange having a half-grown kid now living in your house calling you Dad, but I came to love her like my own and it has stayed that way. I was a little worried at first when Ronni got here because Nora had been the only child to that point, but she proved me wrong 'cause she was great with Ronni. They were inseparable and Ronni loved her some "RaRa", as she called her.

When I divorced, I worried how it might affect Nora after all the things she had put up with and been through in her short life. The way it worked out was she wanted to stay with me and I was more than happy to have it that way. Things were not always golden and anyone who has teenage girls knows that these are trying, hormonal and often difficult times. She was 14 at the time and more than once I considered smothering her in her sleep. Not really, but teenagers have an uncanny ability to jump right on that last nerve of yours with little effort. She must have been related to me somewhere down the line because she had the temper and the mouth that was consistent with my family tree, but on the other hand that was unlikely because she was really good at math and I'm not. Churchill once said, "An army of women and hormones could win any war." Love that man. She and I had our moments, but for the most part we were ok until she decided that my rules didn't need to be followed and went to try out her mom's house for a while. That didn't last long and the next thing I know she had had enough of that bullshit and was living on her own. She later came to me and told me how wrong she had been and was sorry for putting me and Jenny through all that.

Despite our reconciliation, she left school and went back to Alabama, where she met this asshole that I knew was a piece of shit, and married him against my wishes. Why is it our kids never see the wisdom we are trying to impart to them so as not to suffer the same mistakes we did? They just look at you like you just shit in their cornflakes and do it anyway. So anyway, this arrangement lasted about a year or so before the little bastard started screwing around on her. She actually forgave him the first few times and tried to make it right but finally wised up and gave him the boot. I offered to make the little bastard disappear like Jimmy Hoffa but Nora wouldn't go for it, probably because by this point we have a beautiful little grand-girl by the name of Jodie. When I tell you she is gorgeous I'm not just saying it 'cause she's my grandbaby—well, maybe a little. I mean she is beautiful and has "Papa doc", as she calls me, and "Nana Jenny" wrapped around her little finger. I only wish they lived a little closer. Nora did try to amend things with her mom but it never got right. On Thanksgiving one year, they had a big blow out with a knock-down, drag-out fight, complete with hair pulling and the whole nine yards and have not spoken since.

Time passes, as it always does, and in a hurry most of the time. Now Jodie has grown up some and at the time of this writing is about to start school. I guess that explains why I have so many new wrinkles on my face. I'm not sure how or really when it occurred, but another guy, Jerry, showed up in Nora's life and has been there quite some time now. Jerry is a very nice guy, a little odd and kinda nerdish, but I like him and he's good to my girls. That last part is all a father really can ask for, isn't it? As long as someone is good to them and will keep them safe, we can relax a little. Nora went back to school and at present is in nursing school, and I couldn't be more proud of her. I don't keep in touch like I should, even though I think of them daily if not hourly. I always say I need to do better at keeping up with them and something else will get in the way, which is pretty selfish on my part, I think and definitely not an excuse. Ronni does see her sister a few times a year and I try to make sure it stays that way. I don't really have a feel from Ronni on the subject of Rara, but I do know she loves and misses her. I believe when she is old enough she will figure out what we already know and it too will be resolved. Meanwhile we as parents do what we must to keep them whole, safe and secure. Love you guys.

BABY

Now guys, I don't give a fuck how tough you think you may be, women can and will kick your ass anytime they feel like it. It's like bringing a knife to a gun fight; you're going to lose. Women just have a way of taking you by the nut sack and squeezing until you give in—and they do it all without laying a hand on you. Think about it: those bumper stickers you see that say "Girls Rule" just didn't appear at random; someone tested that theory. If you're good with peanut butter sandwiches and sexual self-gratification for the rest of your life then have at it, but not me. They are a necessary evil, gentleman, so get over it because you ain't going through her or around her. I've had this battle on going most of my adult life and have been able to stay alive this long by following three rules: #1. You're wrong no matter what, so just go ahead and admit it right at the start of a disagreement. Repeat as necessary. #2. Repeat after me, "Yes dear, you're right. Gee I wish I'd thought of that." Repeat as necessary. #3. Accept the fact that we can't cook for shit unless it involves charcoal and that we require sexual favors on a regular basis to stay in our right minds, and both of these cards are held by women. Any questions?

Being the hard headed sum-bitch I am, it has taken me three marriages and an unknown number of girlfriends to figure this out. I really thought that I was just not compatible with anyone and I really didn't need to be married or wanted to because relationships just never seemed to go the way I felt it should. They say there is someone for everyone, you just have to find them. Really, how the hell does that work? Well, seeing as y'all are asking, I'm gonna tell you . . . Walmart. No shit, go to Wally world, because that's where I found mine.

I was standing in the aisle by hardware when I first laid eyes on Jenny. I just stood there and I knew in that moment she was the one. I have no idea how I knew I just did. She's standing in the tool section so it's got to be legit, right? She was beautiful and I had no idea who she was or if she was married, lesbian, Amish, Taliban or what. All I could do was just stand there and stare (I may have been drooling also) as she was going out the door, and things are rapidly turning to shit because she got into a Mercedes and drove off. (Ya, I followed her—so what? It wouldn't be the last time I'd do it.) Anyway, I just watched her drive away, not having any idea if I would ever lay eyes on her again. All the time I was thinking, Go *talk to her, asshole.* Nope, no stones to pull that one off, and I just let her go without saying a word. As it happened, luck was in my corner for a change about a week later.

There is this local gym in town where at the time I was teaching martial arts in a few nights a week. The area where the classes were taught was the center part of a running track they had upstairs, and guess who was walking around it that night with her buddies? Yup, none other, and even though she will deny this I know she was looking at me just as much as I was her. I never spoke with her till the next week, and I have Ronni to thank for that. Ronni was two years old and could talk the ear off anyone who would listen. While I was teaching, she was in the daycare area downstairs, and when I went to pick her up she was already out in the hall talking to Jenny about her pink boots. I have no idea what I said to her but it was probably stupid and incomprehensible, and Jen doesn't remember either, probably because it was stupid and incomprehensible. I was nervous as hell—I mean, you couldn't have pulled a pin outta my ass with John Deere. I'll bet I looked like a 40 year old man acting like a teenage moron on his first girl encounter and she probably was thinking, *This boy ain't too right in the head* but was too polite to say so.

From here I went into stalking mode—at least, that's what Jen calls it. I call it doing your homework. I asked people I had seen her talking to that I also knew about who she was, what she did, was she married—you know, the usual profiling stuff. I thought I was done at this point because my investigation had revealed her being in an on/off relationship with a local guy in town that was more off than on, apparently. Nonetheless, it's a solid moral rule of mine that you don't cut another man's lawn while he's sitting on it, if you get my drift. I knew she owned her own business, an assisted living center in town, and I may have driven by it a few times, hoping to catch a glimpse of her . . . but I, uh . . . don't remember. So this goes on for a few weeks and I see her at the gym, talked very briefly to her a few times, nothing serious, until one day everything changed. My sources tell me she is out of her previous relationship and I finally had enough pluck to go to her work and see if she wanted to go out sometime. Now I'm gonna sidetrack here for a moment in the interest of imagery and visual reference. Back then my hair was so long I could sit on it and kept mostly in a ponytail. I wore cowboy boots and jeans (Wranglers, of course) most of the time and a Stetson. Got the image? Good, let's proceed 'cause it gets a little strange from here on out. I stroll into her work, trying to act like it was an accident I ended up here, and at the front desk is this very proper looking elderly lady. I'm thinking it's one of her inmates that lives here so I ask her if I can talk to Ms. Finch. This lady gave me a look and the once-over like she had x-ray vision and had just frisked me for weapons and contraband. She tells me very politely that Jenny's not here; did I want to leave a message. Now I'm thinking, this ole girl is gate-keeping me, so I decide to write a note to her and then for reasons unknown to me, I crumple it up in the trash and tell this lady that I will come back later.

I wasn't there for this next part but apparently when Jenny got back the "ole girl" (we're going to get to her in a minute) told her about my visit and her friend Barbara (Jenny's second mom) fished the note out of the trash can and made her call me. According to Jen, she was not going to nor did she want to call or get involved with the likes of me or any of the male species. Sorry to screw up your plans, hon. I about broke my neck getting to the phone and did my best to sound all casual and shit, like it was no big deal she was calling, and made a date with her for dinner later that night.

So date time rolls around and as I pull up to her place and Barbara comes running, telling me, "Ride around the block a few times, then come back," all kinda secretive and stuff and very weird. So I circle the wagon a few times and pull up in front again. This time Jen comes running out, jumps in the truck, ducks down under the dash and says, "Drive, go, drive." Now, I may be just a good ole Southern boy and admittedly at times not too bright, but I got the distinct impression shit just wasn't right here. I just looked at her, bent over double hiding from God knew who or what, and drove off. We got down the road a ways before I finally said, "Is there something you need to tell me?" It was a few miles down the road like this till she finally sat in the seat and strapped in and I got the explanation. Apparently the dickhead she had been going out with for quite a while wasn't happy with the current arrangement between them and had been stalking her, for lack of a better term. He had somehow come to find out about our little date and was none too happy about it. 'Course she had no clue I had been stalking her also, but even I knew then was not the time to confess that little jewel. Anyway, we headed off to dinner in another town so there was no real chance of stalker boy showing up. Secretly I wish he had. I could have used the exercise but we had a nice evening and an uneventful ride back home.

MaMa

Let me tell you about this "ole girl" I mentioned earlier. I had no idea at the time but this lady was Jen's grandmother, the one who raised her, guided her, cooked fried chicken on Sundays for her and made sure she got the pulley bone, stood by her and loved her without judgment. She was "Mama" (Pronounced Maw-Maw for you Yankees) to us and anyone who knew her. To say this lady was the matriarch of the family was an understatement; she was everything to all of us, especially me. I absolutely adored this lady and my only regret in our relationship was I had not known her longer and spent more time with her when she was still with us. I don't have a clear play by play on how most of this unfolded over the years, but to hear Jen tell it, it always revolved one way or another around Mama.

Jenny's childhood was not what we picture all little girls going through; she had it rough. As she puts it, "Without Mama, things would have come out a lot different and been much worse." Mama was a seamstress, worked in the same sewing factory for 30 years and was married to Buster, a half-blooded Cherokee Indian and from all accounts a real character, but we'll get to him in just a bit. Jen was Mama's favorite; that was obvious to me from the outset. There was a bond between them that was different than with her brother and sister. Her mom and dad divorced when she was about nine or ten years old and Jen's mom was away a lot with her job escorting house trailers or working in the sewing plant. Her daddy, Whirl, worked on the pipeline, so the kids stayed on and off with Mama and Buster a good bit.

Buster wore only overalls that were 2 sizes too big, and I'm told could cure a rainy day with the native herb and plant medicine he knew. Jen says Buster was famous for two things, making chicken and dumplings and growing tomato plants that people would drive from miles around to get. She told me this guy was a real character and I would have gotten along well with him. I'm just sorry I never had that opportunity, as he passed when Jen was in her late twenties.

Jen was the middle of three, between sister Mickie and a younger brother, Jamie—great people, both of them, and I love them to death. Jen says Mickie was the brains and school nerd but it was Jamie who read every encyclopedia in the house. Mick was always studying and getting good grades at school and as siblings will do, Jen used this to her advantage by stealing her sister's car every chance she got. Mickie would be studying and Jen makes off with her car, Nice! Jenny was the athlete: track, basketball, cheerleader and so on. Jamie, on the other hand, was tortured by both of his sisters un-mercifully, bless his heart. They would do things like strap him to his tricycle and roll him down the hill into the briar patch. He would get so pissed he would take off into the woods and be gone for hours. During the times that neither parent was home they were babysat by none other than the Grand Wizard of the KKK. This was not an uncommon thing in those days and as I'm sure you're aware, the Klan was pretty prevalent and highly visible, especially in Mississippi.

There were divorce issues with Jenny's parents and at times things got a little dysfunctional. At the age of about twelve her dad came to pick them up from Mama drunk one day and met up with Buster on the porch with his shot gun. The exact conversation is not known but Jen remembers it something to the effect of "Whirl, get the hell outta here or I'm going to blow your head off. The kids stay here." And they did just that, staying with Buster and Mama on and off till Jen was about 16. By this time the family had moved to a house in the projects and as Jen tells it, "I thought we had moved up to the big time then." From about ages 13-16 Jen lived there and with Mama and somewhere along the line had acquired a beat-up old Volkswagen bug she was driving her and Jamie back and forth to school in. The thing was a piece of shit, with holes in the floor, and would not stay in gear so while she was steering her brother would hold the shifter down so it wouldn't jump outta gear. We've probably all had a few of those in our time.

Before age 12 they lived in a half-built house her daddy started calling "the basement" to the kids. Why the basement? 'Cause that's all that ever got built. It was in the woods about 2 miles from Mama's house, down a mile-long driveway, and was built into the side of a hill. This place apparently was in the constant throes of being built and stayed that way, never being finished. It leaked when it rained, was cold and at any given time it was full of water, scorpions, mold, drunks playing poker, KKK members, assorted critters and three young kids. It certainly wasn't a whole lot better after their parents divorced, but they had Mama and she had them.

Jen's mom Janette and I have a love-hate relationship. Not like she wants to shoot me on sight or anything, just that every chance I get to aggravate her, I never pass it up and she is on me the same way. I love her to death and would do anything in the world for her, and she knows it. After her divorce she remarried a great guy named Harold. His only dysfunction was he was a die-hard Crimson Tide fan. I always told him I could forgive this to some point because he apparently just wasn't raised right. When Jen and I were dating, Harold faked a gout attack so he and Janette could come to the ER when I was working and get an eye full of who was dating their daughter. Imagine my surprise when they dropped that little tidbit on me. Sometime later I went to their house for the first time for dinner and Janette apparently was all in a tizzy about having a "Doctor" at their house. That got fixed real quick after she saw me eat 'cause I always eat like it's the last time I'm gonna ever see food and it's not a pretty sight, believe me.

Harold's passion was Alabama football and hot rods, of which he built some nice ones. About 4 years ago Harold left us for that big football field in the sky and left a huge hole in this family. We love and miss you, Rooster. Janette has bounced back from all this and is doing well with what she loves, buying and selling antiques. There ain't a garage sale, antique store or flea market from Birmingham to Pensacola this woman ain't been in and turned upside down at least once.

I have to share this with y'all to give you an idea the lengths I will go to aggravate her. Janette is always taking shit from me about not going to the doctor and having regular check-ups and so on. What she does is adjusts her own meds and then asks me to call in more when she gets low. She is a huge Alabama fan and loves to shove it in my face when they beat my team, Tennessee. Well, it just so happened that Alabama was playing Auburn and she hates Auburn. The day before the game she called me needing her blood pressure medicine refilled, so guess who had to send me a picture of her wearing a war eagle shirt before I would call in her meds! I know I'm gonna pay for this dearly somewhere down the road, but God, it was soooooo worth it.

Jen had Rhett quite young and ended up married to Rhett's dad by default, who in my humble, biased opinion needs killing. I ain't gonna talk about him 'cause I'll just get pissed off and get to cussing more than I already have. Mama was there for her as always, gentle, kind and wise to guide her through it. Rhett, her son is an awesome kid and Mama also had her hand in that when it came to raising him. Mama made no bones about how she felt about Rhett's dad and another guy that had been in their lives and it was also made very clear to me that I had some measuring up to do in her eyes.

The asshole sperm contributor that was Rhett's dad beat the hell out of Jen the whole time and almost killed her. Not only that, he didn't do shit as a father and screwed around on her while she was at home recovering from her beatings and taking care of the boy. You ever have one of those things where you wish you were there or had been involved in something much earlier on because you're pretty sure you would have fixed it? I do and this is one of them. Jen worked her ass off at three jobs when she finally got back on her own and Mama kept the boy. Jen never asked for anything or took one red cent in government aid. Can't say that about motherfuckers today, can you? They think they're entitled to everything without contributing anything. But I digress—my apologies, it's just something that pisses me off.

My first real get to know session with Mama was a ways into our relationship and boy, talk about getting the once-over. We had gone to see Mama for the weekend and I had gotten up earlier than everyone else, so it was just me and Mama cooking breakfast. In her house there was no coffee and toast in the morning; it was the full court press. If it was in the fridge and cookable, it was on the table. She spent the next hour telling me all kinds of things that were on her mind and why they were there. She would never cuss or raise her voice; she didn't threaten or try to intimidate me either, she was just Mama. She spoke, you listened and you minded. She and the Lord were on a first-name basis, and you can just bet that every Sunday the Lord got him an ear full too. She just commanded a presence that made you hang on every word she said. That morning, buddy, she very much in her way let me know that I was on notice as far as Jenny was concerned. Basically, it wouldn't go well for me if I got out of line.

We moved to Mississippi not too long after we got married, and of all the reasons to stay in Alabama, Mama was the only real one. We visited her as often as we could but as usual hind ight is always perfect and maybe we could have done better. I came to know and love this lady a great deal in a very short time. We got the call one day from Jenny's brother that she had been found in her house, unresponsive for an unknown amount of time. She never regained consciousness from a stroke and within a week she was gone. This is one of those times where you just have to get past the guilt first: the self-inflicted guilt of not being there for her, letting her go through that alone, hoping she was not in pain and wishing you had spent more time with her. All of it normal and human, none of it relevant. The fact is, being there or not, the results would have been the same. I miss you, Mama, and love you always.

Rhett

I met Rhett when he had just turned 21 and his mom and I were drunk as hell, which ranks up there with stupid for great first impression to the potential stepson. He apparently wasn't too happy with me because I went to him to ask if I could marry his mom some months later and he said no but I did it anyway. Nah . . . Just shitting you, he gave me the nod; however, I've never asked him if he ever regretted it. He was already grown and married to his wife and I missed all that, damn. In a lot of ways he and are alike and some say we even favor each other. He and his mom are identical in their ways and it's funny because they can't work on the same project long together without wanting to kill one another. They are so much alike and "AA" personalities that they bang heads. Jen is one of those who wants to have it her way—and hardheaded, my God, she is hardheaded. Rhett and I are also, just not to the degree she is. I think a lot of the way she is stems from her being on her own and raising Rhett because she relied on no one, had to be strong and pick her own self up by the bootstraps 'cause no one else was going to do it for her. This sort of brings me to her second husband and another asshole that needed killing.

She was married about 10 years to this guy and hated every minute of it. When I talked to her about it and asked her why she stayed, she told me she had nowhere else to go and at least Rhett had a stable environment. "I didn't know any better" is what she would say. As it turned out, it was Rhett who made the decision for them to get the fuck out of Dodge. He hated this guy because he was mean and hard on Rhett every chance he got. In a way you have to know Rhett to understand this next part but it basically it came down to him having had enough of this asshole when he was about 16. It all started over him wanting to go to the skating rink with his friends after he had worked all day to make the money to go, and this guy wouldn't let him go out of spite. He and Rhett got into it and he made the mistake of putting his hands on Rhett again and Rhett lost it. From what I understand, if his mom had not pulled him off there is no telling what he would have done to this guy. Needless to say, this chapter was closed in a hurry and they moved out to their own place.

Rhett is what my dad would have called "the ones you watch out for". This boy is quiet and soft-spoken, polite, and always does his best to do the right thing, regardless of consequence. But you get on the wrong side of him and you best be ready, because he becomes a person you don't want a piece of. It's a stretch to get him that way but brother, once he's there it's on. To put this in perspective, he and his wife at the time rented this place from some folks and they were less than appropriate in the way they did business and basically harassed the shit out of them for one thing or another. Well, one morning this ole boy calls up Rhett's wife and starts threatening her on the phone about something. Rhett takes the phone and listens to this guy's bullshit for a while and tells him several times to watch his mouth. Apparently he wasn't paying attention cause the next thing outta Rhett's mouth was "Boy, you had best watch your mouth or I'll come down there and beat your ass before I go to work!" Evidently this asshole got the hint and backed off. He had no idea how close he came to getting a big ole can of whoop ass opened up on him.

Rhett and I have never been what I would call super close—by that I mean like him and his mom. I love him like he is my own and would do anything in the world for him, always will. What we do have, though, is a good understanding of each other. He, I'm sure, loves me too, as best as he knows how for a kid who has had a lot of major disappointment in his life from the male species. I mentioned earlier that his sperm donor was never a dad or a father to the boy and Rhett never saw him for most of his life. Rhett has nothing to do with his birth father anymore and I think a lot of that has to do with finding out what he did to his mom when he was a baby. Things he has only recently found out. A couple of years ago his dad tried to get back more in Rhett's life and Rhett just finally told him to basically fuck off. He told him, "You have never been there before; what makes you think you can come back now? I have a dad and it ain't you." The only real male figures in his life till I showed up were his Uncle Jamie and Paw Paw Whirl. On a daily basis growing up, it was his mom being both parents most if not all the time. His Paw Paw passed about 7 years ago and I think it hurt him more than he has let on.

I have done my best to be a good dad and father to him, but Rhett has always kept me to some degree, at arm's length which is perfectly understandable. I'm good with that, son, just so you are in my life and I can continue to love you the way I do. He and I think a lot the same on things and when he does ask me my opinion we are usually pretty close in our thinking.

He recently divorced his wife but he has a beautiful boy, Grayson, to show for it. I always wished he had had a girl 'cause then he would really know what it's like to have your ass whipped by a girl. But we have Grayson and wouldn't take nothing for him. Rhett is a great dad and I'm sure he wants to be all the things his was not. Every day that grandboy of mine does something to amaze us all or make us laugh like hell. He is very smart and has his Paw Paw Whirl's memory 'cause he don't forget shit.

Like his mom, Rhett has a very unique personality quirk that I wish I could have just a taste of. He has never met someone who just didn't like him. He has a natural way with folks that people love and cling to. His mom is the same way; she walks into a room and everyone wants to know who she is. He has more friends than he can shake a stick at, and most he has had since he was a little boy. It is even worse with the women because he is a good looking guy, a gentleman and never short of female company. The cool thing is he treats them like ladies and not like just another girl, which I think is one of the reasons they stay on him like they do. His mom taught him that.

As I have already proclaimed to y'all, this boy can build some shit. A few years ago he decided that, as he put it, "I don't want to swing a hammer the rest of my life" so he opened a BBQ restaurant. He had never cooked BBQ in his life till he opened the door for business and the folks around town loved it and he did fairly well. Personally, I'm not a big BBQ fan on the best of days but man, that kid changed my mind in a hurry. Still to this day the best BBQ I have ever eaten, and I'm not saying that because he's my son; I wouldn't do that to him or you. He had some kind of rub he developed and a sauce to go with it that just made the difference. He sold that business last year and he and his mom built an oyster bar (The High Tide Oyster bar) that is about to open its doors. What do they know about cooking oysters? Not a damn thing but I'd bet you they're going to be awesome. I'd lay money on it 'cause that's just how those two are when they get in the mind of something. Me, I'd probably look for a book on it but not those two: head first all the way. So if you're ever down Gulf Shores, Alabama way, drop by and say hello.

Jen never got married again until we did. She dated and even lived with a guy for a very brief while but she said it was not what she wanted or was looking for. The guy was apparently ok to her and Rhett but had other issues, like drugs and alcohol. I gather it was an on and off again relationship and to be honest, I never asked her much about details, I guess 'cause I just didn't want to know. When I met her she told me that there was no way she was going to get involved with me, that she had decided to be a lesbian and was fixing to pack her shit and be gone to Florida. How'd that work out for ya, hon? The guy she dated owned a construction company and Rhett worked for him a long time. This is where he learned to be a carpenter and builder and when I tell you this kid is an awesome builder, it's a no-shit fact; ask anyone he's done work for. There is nothing that kid can't build. I mean anything. He does quality work too, because he is so picky about it. I will guarantee it will be exact, no mistakes—that's how he works. Anyway y'all, that's about all I have to say about my boy; he's just one of those people you have to meet to believe it and a huge part of my heart. Love you, son.

The rest of the Story

Jen and I started to date some, and I ended up at some point in the road asking her what she was doing the rest of my life. Somewhere in all this we had taken to calling each other "baby" and just how this came about I don't know but it continues the same today. We had decided to just go to the courthouse and do the "I do and she does" thing—at least, that's what she thought we had decided, but I had other plans. Unknown to her I had worked it out so that a friend of mine who owed a little wedding chapel had it set for us to be wed there. I picked her up that morning and went to the court office where I went in first, hung out for a few minutes then went back out telling her that there was a problem and we would have to come back when the Justice of the Peace returned. So off we went back home, or so she thought. On the way I told her I had a little surprise but wouldn't tell her what it was 'cause she hates not knowing something and I was revving her up on purpose. I kept this up and she was getting really pissed as I pulled up to this little chapel and right away she sees her friends, family, Mama and my mom and it hits her. She's crying, I'm crying (ya, I cry, ok? It's acceptable in this day and age.) and of course she's not pissed anymore. It went well, and was certainly one of the highlights in my life that I scored major points on.

About 8 years ago she decided that she wanted to sell real estate so she went and got her license. It wasn't too long after that the ass fell out of the market and you couldn't give a fucking house away. So what does she do? She starts her own construction company with my son and one of their first projects was a two acre strip mall. There have been others, like the restaurant they are about to open, but that was a big one and she could be found right in there with the boys in her jeans and flip flops digging and a hammering. You aint seen nothing like it, folks, believe me—at one point she had more calluses on her hands than I did and bitched like hell cause her nails got trashed.

I won't tell you we haven't had our moments over the years 'cause there have been a few—well, a bunch—but then again, she has put up with an awful lot of my bullshit over the years (and I hers). That's marriage, ain't it? I reckon I'm not ready to pitch her out just yet because I'd be hard pressed to find another like her. Just because I got her at Walmart doesn't mean there's another on the shelf. On any given day it seems she's zigging while I'm zagging and we are both going full throttle from daylight to dark. She's just as gorgeous as the first day I laid eyes on her, and I definitely ain't giving that up. We don't have a lot of likes and hobbies in common most of the time, but that works too because the things we do have in common we do together as much as possible and all our kids seem to be happy and healthy. When it comes down to it, you can't ask for more than that, now can you? Love you, baby.

The Military

I once saw a picture of a soldier in a helicopter, obviously hurt and in deep medical trouble from a mission he was fighting in. On his chest were tattooed these words: *"For those I love I will sacrifice everything"*. I had to give this chapter some serious thought before I sat down to do it and that soldier justice. How do we honor soldiers like this one? You and I have never met him or shook his hand, although I'm sure we would be honored to do so. These warriors are the heart and soul of the military and the epitome of what a soldier represents to those of us serving and to civilians who truly care what happens to these guys.

We won't be here long because what I have to say will be to the point. I will start by saying this, serving in the military with people like that soldier is the single most important thing I have done in my life. I have a pride and a strength ingrained in me because of my service that has made me a better person, and by default I think a better doctor, cop and father. I cannot express this to you in any other way but that, and I wish everyone could have that kind of education. If I had the power to make it so, everyone physically able would do 2 years of active service right out of high school. I guarantee you it would cure a good portion of the shit our youth of today does and acts like.

I come from a long line of people who have served and been proud to do so. It was because of them and other realistic reasons that I did the same—my father being an obvious one. The military has given and taken from me and those before me, sometimes more than we wanted to pay, but this is the price we agreed to when we signed up. It's the cost of doing business, the price of freedom, democracy and the comfort of going to bed each night knowing someone out there has your back and is the keeper of the watch. There is a certain ambiance that surrounds the people and the families of those who serve. A knowing and sharing of unspoken things that are only really understood in the brotherhood of the military. This is all the more self-evident in those of us who have seen combat because the lessons taught there are for the rest of your life, clear and unforgiving in their message.

Some of the greatest advancements in medicine, engineering and aviation are because of the military and usually at the cost of war. Throughout history in this country, the military has remained one of the constants relied on to protect its people and the laws and beliefs for which they stand for over 250 years. I have not always agreed with the politics and the stands of our government, particularly when it comes to fighting a war, but that is irrelevant; I am a soldier and I follow orders. Do I think that some asshole politician with his lawyer flunky should be dictating procedures and policy on the battle field? Hell no! That kind of shit and stupidity has cost the lives of numerous American soldiers in several conflicts. You can't have someone without eyes on the battleground giving you orders in the field; it's absurd and dangerous. But it happens more than you are probably aware of. Just because it's on CNN doesn't mean it's the truth or all of the story. Talk to a vet and ask him or her how many dumbass orders they were given by others on the other side of the world or how the ROE (rules of engagement) are governed by Washington lawyers; they'll tell you. They will also tell you this: "I'm a soldier and I follow orders and regardless of where they come from I will carry them out without question".

I hear a lot these days from people and the press about how we as a country are sick of war and we need to leave and let them sort themselves out. Really? Well, not to rain on anyone's party but that's how we got into this in the first place, remember? They came here and fucked with us first, so how long do you think it will be, if left to their own devices, before they do it again? These idiots are zealots and will not quit for any reason, I can guarantee you this. It's easy for us to Monday morning quarterback this war based on what these bullshit artists we call the press and their so-called experts say on CNN. The truth is, unless you are in the shit and boots on the ground down range you don't have a frigging clue what you're talking about. There will be some who read this saying the same about me, I'm sure and that's fine. They are entitled to feel that way and I give even less of a shit. I know firsthand what I'm talking about and I'm not tired of war, just the way we are going about it. The public are not asking the right questions and are not being given truthful answers to the ones they do ask.

The facts are these: without the military we could all be speaking Japanese or German and before that maybe Spanish. Soldiers don't sign up for the pay; their motivation is they are patriots and believe in us as a country and what we stand for. They are prepared to pay the ultimate sacrifice with no fear or hesitation, as thousands have already done in one campaign or another. How do you measure that or pay that forward? By supporting and taking care of the ones who have served, suffered and are still here, that's how. Putting a yellow ribbon on the trunk of your car don't mean shit to the soldier trying to learn how to live without his arm or a leg or both.

On the news the other day because of a government shutdown (What other country have you ever heard do that?) they closed the WWII memorials to visitors. I see these veterans in wheelchairs waiting to be let in to a place they made possible and they would not let them. Finally, a few of them basically said fuck you, we're going in and they did. It's that kind of attitude that allowed us to prevail in that war and others since. I was so proud of them and that's exactly what I would have done. So you tell me, who's wrong here? If you can believe this, some bureaucratic asshole talked about handing out trespassing charges to these soldiers. Really? I'd buy a ticket to that fight because he would have had such a shit storm to deal with it would have been fun to watch him get his head shoved up his ass. Of course nothing happened, but as usual you can count on having at least one bureaucratic asshole in the crowd.

We owe these people a debt that could never be paid and is not expected to be. I was walking through Walmart the other day with my uniform on and this old man stopped me and wanted to shake my hand and thank me for doing my part in the service. This happens a lot to soldiers these days and it is very nice of people to express their appreciation. That day this man was wearing a cap that said *"USS*

Arizona Veteran". Ring a bell? Ya, that USS Arizona. I talked to him a while about the horror of that long ago December morning. He said he did not blame or carry ill will to anybody about it. He said, "It was just war." What he did say and I will never forget was this: "I thought I would never see our country that angry ever again. I guess I was wrong." There were officially only 334 survivors on that ship; today there are only about 20 or so still with us. With these warriors dies an era and a world they lived in that we can only read about in books. In my humble opinion, meeting this man in Walmart that day goes down in my holy shit column and I was truly blessed and honored to have had that opportunity.

The bottom line is this, folks, we are soldiers and we go where we are told and do what we are told without question. To those of you who are tired of the war, I understand, but it's not the soldiers' fault, which was the mentality of the nation about those who went to Vietnam. Most didn't want to go, but go they did because they were soldiers. Calling them baby killers and a ream of other not-so-nice things was ridiculous and absolutely absurd. It was war and they were soldiers.

I for one will continue to wear this uniform as long as they will let me. We rely on our military to help us in times of disaster, fight for us in times of war and protect us from those who would harm us or our way of life. A huge undertaking any way you look at it, but it has been this way for over 250 years and is not about to change anytime soon. They do a job most would not want to and they do it with honor, courage and integrity. This I believe, as I'm sure most of you do, demands our prayers, support and respect at the very least.

May God bless and protect our military, home and abroad. Hooorah!

RANTS

I wasn't going to do this chapter originally but I could not bring myself to ignore it. It is going to be so much fun because I get to bitch, moan and whine while passing on opinions on anything I want, with no one telling me to shut my pie hole. My wife usually just looks at me like I have a dick in the middle of my forehead, gets disgusted or bored, and walks away. Y'all will probably do the same and I can't really blame you if none of the things I am about to embark upon mean anything to you.

So what's a rant? This is where I pick on something that is either really pissing me, the rest of the world or both off to no end. I mean like getting on my last nerve kinda pissed off. I get to express my dislike or total disgust as loudly as I can while simultaneously voicing my own petty opinion on the matter. It can be very therapeutic but will never replace sex and cold beer in the feel-good department. What follows here are a small collection of experiences, observations and opinions that are mine and mine alone. If you find yourself agreeing, that's great; if you don't, well, I really don't give a shit. I tend not to let a lot of things get under my skin and as I get on in years, even less does, mostly because I have come to the conclusion that it's not going to change, at least not in my lifetime so why get upset with it. I will, however, crusade for it if I feel strongly enough there is a chance it will change for the better or I have some form of influence upon it for my children and grandchildren's sake. So with that said, let's dance.

Government Handouts

I picked this one to go first because overall it is probably to one that irritates me the most. Why is that? Well, it may be that every time I go to work I get it put in my face. Young people, for the most part, hooked on pain medication, seeking more and trying to get anything else they can for nothing. These sorry motherfuckers are just above plankton on the food chain and some are not worth the air they use up. I know there are legitimate cases of people who truly need help, and I will be the first one in line to give it but for the most part they are the minority. Just because you're depressed, have back pain or some other bullshit excuse doesn't mean you should be allowed to sit at home all day playing with yourself and the Xbox. You can answer a phone, stuff envelopes, do something.

Last year I'm working in the ER and I go in this room where there is this 20-something year old guy in the room cuddled up with his girlfriend on the gurney wearing camo fatigues used by hunters and giggling away like some three year old. So he tells me he's here because his back hurts and he has chronic back problems, is on disability for his back and is on chronic pain meds every day through a pain management office. I look at what he's taking and I am blown away. You name it, he's on it and at this visit he can hardly talk he is so loaded. Then he tells me he hurt his back again deer hunting this weekend. Then he says, and I shit you not, "Give me the good stuff, doc, I have Medicare and Medicaid." Really, asshole?! Who the hell do you think is paying for you to sit at home and do nothing? But you can go deer hunting while I'm here busting my ass to give the government my money I earned working so you can stroke your trash girlfriend and sit there telling me to give you the good stuff! Are you out of your ever-loving mind? You can guess how the rest of the visit went. This, folks, is all the time and I can't even begin to tell you how many of these I see on a daily basis. My wife's friend gets over $3000/month from the government to sit her fat ass at home with Medicare because she is "depressed". Ya, that's what I said, depressed.

I don't blame her or the other assholes just like her, really; they just fill out the paperwork. I blame the government because there is no consequence or gatekeeper to this shit. You have some government contracted civilian doctor that gets paid by the number of patients he sees and just runs them through like cattle. Who checks on him? The dumbass clerk they just hired off the Kentucky Fried Chicken production line? Genius, just fucking genius. Most of these folks couldn't find their ass in a closet with both hands. Where do they get off handing our money that we busted our ass for to the dickheads in the crowd?

This friend of mine worked hard his whole life, served in the Gulf War, saved his money and planned his retirement. Last year he gets sick with cancer. His insurance company drops him under some fine print clause (we'll get to these pricks later). Now he is stuck with paying all his bills out of what he has saved and it didn't take long to get drained, as you can imagine. He is about to lose everything so he goes to his government, our government, you know—of the people, for the people, for some help. They basically tell him no way because you have a job. In other words fuck you, get back to work so these other lazy fuck-sticks can get their shit free. He has kids and bills and then some so he decides to try taking care of himself holistically to try and lessen some of his financial burden. Soon enough, shit got out of control, he ends up in hospital and dies 2 weeks later. Now his family has no money, no provider, no dad, no husband and some huge-ass medical bills. The government still said fuck you based on some dumb shit reasoning, even for an EBT card. The wife files for bankruptcy 'cause she really has no other choice. They lose the house and everything and now live in some dumpy-ass trailer in a shit neighborhood and the kids had to change schools. Mom has two kids and a minimum wage job trying to make it and here is the part that really pisses me off. She tells me that while she's in this office trying to get signed up for food stamps, this skank-looking, smelly and obviously intoxicated woman comes in and they take her back and sign her up. She just got out of jail a month ago for prostitution. (The skank told her this like it was some huge career move.) She also tells her that she gets $200/week "displaced persons" money. What? What the fuck is that? She never found out and I cannot find it on any government website. If anyone out there finds it, please send it to me at the email address in the back.

This, my friends, is how our country and government works now. The less productive and more of a lazy, freeloading asshole you are, the more we will give you: a place to live, food, medical insurance and you know what, just because we have a few extra million laying around this year, we will even give you a cell phone and a ride to the ER for some bullshit reason so you can get your pain med fix. Make sure you call ahead on your free phone to the ER to find out if there is a wait; then you won't have to take time out of your busy day to go to administration and file a complaint about how poor the service was.

You see, those of us who work and pay taxes support this kind of behavior because we elected the politicians doing this, and are allowing it to happen. So you would think that if it's your contributions making all this available, you should be entitled to some, right? Negative. You don't get shit but you do get shit on. The more you contribute, the more they want and take. Government of the people, for the assholes, by the assholes. If I sound angry that's because I am. I was shown a very accurate and truthful statement once that I would like to share:

> *You cannot legislate the poor into freedom by legislating the wealthy out of freedom. What one person receives without working for, another person must work for without receiving. The government can't give to anybody anything that the government does not first take from somebody. When half the people get the idea they don't have to work because the other half's going to take care of them, and the other half get the idea it does no good to work because somebody's going to get what I work for, then that, dear friends, is about the end of any nation.—Dr. A. Rogers.*

I'm pretty sure I am not the only one who has never taken one red cent from the government. No, wait a minute, I lied. There was that time I served my country in the military when we were at war and was paid as a soldier. Does that count? Nah, probably not. I saw an interview on the TV one day and the story was about a Marine whose friend, also a Marine, had his legs and one arm blown off by an IED in Iraq. This Marine had built a special harness, much like the papoose we see carrying babies on the chests of their parents. He would put his friend in it on his back to get him in and out cars, walking around a mall and a few other things. He cared for his friend 24/7. When the interviewer asked him why he did this, the Marine said, "Because he's a Marine, he's my brother and he would do the same for me". I wonder how many of you that are a debt, a burden and a cancer to society would do that, or even understand what that means. He did and he gave it all. What have you done?

BLACK and WHITE

Growing up I was surrounded by the KKK. Klanners were just part of the social hierarchy and way of life in the South. Strangely enough, though, the word "Nigger" was a taboo in our house and has been so in all generations since and before. I know you're thinking well how can you be a Klanner if that word is not used? Well, here is how it was explained to me. The use and abuse of that word are consistent with the rhetoric of the Klan and it is just plain derogatory and according to my family's opinion, wrong and unchristian. I couldn't agree more.

This whole thing is a very complex, volatile and emotional issue that has been fought over and dealt with for 200 years. The reality is we are not any farther ahead now than back then. It's one thing to call someone an asshole, dickhead, jerk or a fuck-stick; those are generic adjectives that are cross-cultural and used for the most part the same in any language or country. Pick a country and they will have similar terms of endearment; the US of A does not have sole rights to profanity. What we do have is the persistence of discrimination on both sides of the fence. If it's not about blacks, it's the Mexicans; if it's not the Mexicans, it's the Orientals and so on. If you think I'm full of shit then pick up the paper or listen to the news: on any given day there will be a race story in there. Test me, I dare you. We are not the only ones with prejudice as an inherent piece of our culture. Jews are still persecuted by non-Jews, Muslim factions are still at war with each other, Pakistanis and Indians still have a longstanding feud that is centuries long. To be honest, our black and white battles are pretty calm, comparatively speaking.

Here is the part that pisses me off to no end. We as white people cannot say the word nigger to or around a black person. That is a big-ass no-no 'cause now you're just a racist trying to keep the white man on top of the black man. What a load of horse shit. Blacks can, however, in their music, to each other, and in anger to white and non-white people say nigger all day long and every other word. This infuriated and puzzled me so much I called Abraham, a friend of mine for many years and blacker than a coal miner's asshole, to ask him why it's ok for blacks to say it even in a derogatory way to each other but a white cannot. You know what he says? "I have been wondering the same thing myself— stupid, ain't it?" He says, "The best I can figure is if they are an asshole, or they like the person, or they are ghetto rats they can use it as a sort of good ole boy language." Huh? WTF does that mean? I have asked other black folks the same question over the years and I get a different answer every time.

I think it's a convenience word. By that I mean it's used to show us they are different and we are not included. They use it with each other to describe the kind of person they're addressing but the fact is there is no reason to use it at all anymore, other than to call someone an asshole, dickhead or whatever. None of them are right but the difference is nigger has a history and a stigma attached to it, one that we as a nation of multicultural facets have to learn to get over. There is no slavery as it was 200 years ago but we are still slaves to our language, social in-acceptance and our persecutions. You keep picking the scab off and it will continue to bleed and never heal.

Martin Luther King was one of the greatest humanitarians that ever lived and one of my personal heroes, not 'cause he was black, but because he stood for something unconditionally and paid for it with his life. I would be willing to bet if you could ask him then about why he was killed he would say something like, "It was necessary for us to heal." What do you think he would say today, nearly 60 years later? How about, "Have you learned nothing from me or from history?" or maybe "This is what I gave my life for?" It's all speculation on my part, but I have read and studied the man enough to know that walking around still using "nigger" on both sides of the color fence was not what he had in mind or wanted for us.

About every year I get detailed as a police officer on a Martin Luther King parade through town. Last year I see these two black guys in the parade who have been arrested at times for one reason or another. What struck me about these two is they are probably the biggest racists

I know of. They hate white people and have said so publicly, but here they are in this parade, grinning like they fucking won something being damn hypocrites. I see these people still hating for color and it sickens me. Generation after generation without any letup. Then you have dumbass white scholars saying stupid shit like, "Because of the shape of the black's skull, his brain is smaller and therefore he has an inferior intellect and always will because of genetics." Really mother fucker, you should see the shape of my grape; that would put your theory in the toilet.

There are a handful of prominent black people who you only seem to see on the TV when there has been some alleged racial act that has made it to page one of the news. They get on the set and talk about racial inequality and keeping the black man as a second class citizen by not giving them the same advantages as whitey. Really? Well, what do you say we have us a little parley on some statistics?

As of a few years ago black genocide was up about a third from previous numbers. That means that blacks kill more blacks than anyone else put together. They also have the highest rate of death and or murder with a firearm. Unemployment was highest among whites but blacks used more of the government programs than anyone else. Whites had the highest rate of teenage pregnancies; blacks had the youngest ages of the same. Whites had the highest usage and arrest for drugs. Blacks had the highest arrest rate for trafficking, right after the Hispanic population. And finally, blacks have the highest rate of gang related crimes by far. My point here is not to point, but to say when does it stop. Why don't these prominent public figures take the same amount of energy and instead of pointing the finger to blame, use it to save some of this generation, black and white? In a lot of ways we are worse off than those days when King marched into Washington, DC and told the world, "I have a dream." You don't give the Nobel Peace prize to a man who is all wrong in his thinking and his methods.

I owe my life to a nigger that some years ago pulled my sorry white ass out of a burning building so one day I could sit down and rant about this. Ray remains still one of my closest friends and no amount of thank you or bottles of his favorite Jack Daniels will ever repay that debt. He knows it and so do I. He neither reminds me about it nor uses it as leverage when he needs me for something, because he knows he merely has to ask. I love his family like they're my own and I would protect them with my life as he has done for me, and none of it has to do with color.

I have saved the lives of hundreds of black, white, yellow, and red people in my careers, and I have never once looked at them as color but as people who needed me and what I was able to do for them. I couldn't give a shit what flavor you are; you'll get exactly the same attention and care. I can't tell you the number of times I have arrested a black person and got the "you're just doing this because I'm black" speech. No, fuck-tard, it's because you broke the law and there is no color in that. My kids were raised the same as I was and I never would allow racial talk in my house period, no exceptions. They know the consequences are right up there with lying and stealing, and I wish I could say the same for others. The sad facts are that as long as there are these radical hate factions like the KKK and white supremacists around to influence our younger generations, we are destined to continue the mistakes of our forefathers. We will continue to be the niggers we have always been, with no end in sight.

Religion

Now before anyone starts pitching a fit, thinking I'm gonna go off on God and start speaking in ancient tongues, reign it back a tad 'cause that's not the case. What I am gonna do is exercise my right to the First Amendment and tell you a few of my thoughts and observations on this subject. I said MY thoughts—not anyone else's, just mine. If you don't agree with what I say, well, good for you; that is your right and I cannot nor will I fault you for that. I will however, support your view and defend it to the best of my ability. This is the oath I took to proudly wear the uniform of the United States Army.

Religion is one of those older than dirt debates and discussions that is right up there with abortion, racism and who shot JR on *Dallas*. Wars have been fought over and because of religious beliefs and its differences for thousands of years. Even today religious difference is the number one catalyst to death, destruction, terror, homicide, war, and genocide in this so called modern era. The bottom line is this: there is no right answer, just your opinion based on your upbringing, exposure and beliefs. All of them are legit and hold the same amount of water as any other.

I was raised Catholic and hated every minute of it. I don't mean the religion itself (although this too has some serious issues); I'm talking about having it shoved down my pie hole throughout my childhood. I was made to attend church every Sunday, whether I wanted to or not. Now folks, if you have ever sat through a Catholic service you will already be shaking your heads going oh, that poor boy. It just sucked and there were always these obnoxious smells in the church, no matter which one you were in. They must have had an order from the Pope or something that says they have to all smell the same way. The incense smell made me a little queasy and always uncomfortable. I was never at ease in church and always wanted to run down the aisle screaming at the top my lungs, "Satan is coming; run for your lives!" or something like that—you get the drift. My parents and grandparents made me go and always gave me the caveat of "one day you will make up your own mind on God and religion but right now you'll do it my way." I did not grow up hating church or begin dancing naked around the bonfire chanting for an animal sacrifice, I just never saw what others saw. I was never "saved", as the Christians put it. So frigging what, I'm happy just the way I am and you are the way you are, right?

I believe it's wrong to steal, lie, murder, and covet thy neighbor's spouse and so on. All ten of the commandments make perfect sense to me and I do my best to follow them and pass them along to my kids and guess what? I didn't have to be religious or a Bible-thumping Christian to understand those concepts. All I had to do was know what was right and wrong.

I believe in the big bang, not Adam and Eve and the whole apple and rib thing. Science has proved more about what and where we came from than the Bible could ever explain. God didn't create the whole shebang in six days; we did, along with good ole Mother Nature over several billion years of earthquakes, meteors, floods and genetic diversity. I'll bet you Baptist types are about ready to set me on fire, aren't ya? Believe me, I am not saying any of this to start the next crusades or be the anti-Christ, I just want my opinion and those like mine heard.

I think it is somehow programmed into us that everyone has to have someone and something to believe in so they can reach for this strength when it really counts and they need it the most. Your strength is not necessarily another's strength and that needs to be respected equally but often is not. I have been called everything from atheist to a heathen devil child because of my arguments, thoughts and points of view on religion, God and the belief in these entities. To counter these opinions and for the sake of debate, I have read the Bible twice, the Koran once and a few others on recorded accounts of things like Hindu and Shinto beliefs. I found them to be very entertaining and I see their points of view but I don't take it on face value, any more than a Buddhist would believe in the Church of England. Nonetheless, religion and believing is held in undeniably high regard and worship for what it stands for and the peace and guidance it gives to those who entertain it. For those of you who have been "saved", I respect that and will defend its honor.

Here is what I have no time or respect for: people who try to shove their beliefs on others and then defile them as sinners and heathens if they choose not to. I despise and detest people who use religion as a platform to launch dissent or political views to further their cause. There are those who use religion and people's faith in the same to accumulate personal wealth and power and abuse that power on the unknowing and the beguiled. And lastly, the one that really pisses me off, those who hide behind their own interpretations of religious scripture then choose, to wreak harm, terror, genocide, and mayhem on others because you don't believe or live as they do and use it as a tool of war. I don't have to spell that one out; y'all know exactly what I'm talking about.

The truth of it is that there is no other option in most religions but to believe in only their religion completely and unquestioningly. Islam is the example I will give at this point because it is allegedly the oldest and definitely the one with most violence and single-mindedness associated with it presently. Pick your religion; I don't care what it is— Catholic, Protestant, Jewish, Methodist, Baptist, Muslim, Buddhist, Mormon, Jehovah witness, Hindu and so on—they all have one belief in common: they are the true religion and source of deity. They all have the ancient scriptures to back this statement up and this is one of the reasons there have been so many wars and murders in the name of these religions. You don't think so? Ok, test time: Name one religion that has never been to war over their beliefs. Answer: There isn't one.

I can get online and get a tax ID number for a nonprofit organization and call it "The church of the left handed bicycle wrench" and presto! A new religion based on my unwavering faith in the left handed bicycle wrench is birthed with little fanfare but just as legit as the Catholic Church or a Mosque. Why? Because the First Amendment says I can. All I need now is a few dumbasses to believe the same as me or just need a cause to thrust themselves into and I will have a following. Being the charismatic fella that I am, I become the guru to this band of merry men and all that follow me. Eventually the enthusiasm of my newfound beliefs starts getting off the path and into the ditch a little bit. I propose that anyone who doesn't believe in the power of left handed wrenches has no place in this world and should be removed because we are the true believers and they are the infidel. I think you see where this is going—sound familiar? The whole scenario is crazier than a run-over dog. Ask Jim Jones; he would tell you if he hadn't liked Kool-Aid so much, but if you can't reach Jim, try one of the thirty-eight from the Heaven's Gate society.

I suppose when it's all said and done, I just wish we as a world could accept each other as we are, where we are and all the baggage that comes with us. I am again reminded of Chief Tecumseh and his words, written over a hundred years ago that in my heart ring so true: "Trouble no one about their religion. Respect others in their view, and demand that they respect yours." Maybe one day.

ADD

A few words on ADD (Attention Deficit Disorder). Bullshit, bullshit and more bullshit. I had never heard of this till med school. OMG, when the fuck are parents going to learn the three rules for raising a kid or kids? 1. If it merits an ass whooping, it gets it. 2. I only tell you once. 3. This not a democracy; what I say goes—end of discussion. Hence the phrase all parents eventually spew out to their kids: "Because I said so, that's why." The attention deficit is not in the child; it's in the parents. I'm here to tell you, if my dad or John Paul spoke, I paid all kinds of attention because any lapse in same was my ass. Today we have gotten away from this and we have become more touchy-feely about discipline. We "Talk", we "Reason", we "Communicate in an effective manner" . . . ahhh, horse shit. Most of the kids these days, especially teens, couldn't tell their ass from page four. I have seen kids tell their parents, "If you touch me I will call DCS." I can just imagine me telling John Paul or my dad, "If you spank me I'm calling child protective services" and right after I regained conscious and they stopped laughing, I would have time to reflect on that idea.

As a kid I was about as hyper as they get and I didn't take medicine to keep me under control because all it took was my parents giving me that look and buddy, I got squared away in a hurry and there was no asking, either. On some discipline my dad and John Paul were over the top, granted, and that cycle and way of doing it has stopped with me. I have whooped my kids but not the way my dad did. If they don't want to mind, then get their frigging attention—it isn't rocket science. Teachers can be the worst when it comes to wanting to medicate. I can't tell you the number of times I have a parent in my clinic telling me the school wants him on medicine because he won't do his work or settle down and be quiet in class. In my day we had a cure for that; it was called the principal's office and the paddle. Teachers have large classes, poor pay and long hours. I know, I was one for a few years. Nonetheless, a class of zombies is not the answer, either. It starts at home because it's easier to give a pill than get in the kid's face and make them mind, so if the parents want to go the easy route, why shouldn't the teachers?

Attention deficit and hyperactivity are real conditions and require real intervention. But the last thing you reach for is medication, not the first. You don't eat a spoon of coffee then drink hot water behind it, now do you? It has become the socially accepted norm to have your child on medication if things don't quite go the way they should at school or home. I saw an interesting article once that showed a time line of when ADD started its rise to prominence and compared it to when martial discipline was removed from the schools and homes. Guess what, my parental readers, they coincided almost exactly!

I am not in any way saying go home and beat your kid every time he or she farts in the wrong company but I am saying that this form of discipline is valid and has been demonstrated through the ages, including in the Bible, to work. In the right measure and circumstance it is necessary and warranted. I'm pretty sure some of you right wingers and tree huggers reading this right now are having a fucking cow over what I have said. Oh well, check the First Amendment; it says I can say this shit and if you don't like it, write your own book. That's all I've got to say about that.

THE LAW

I had to think a minute before I wrote this rant 'cause of several reasons, not the least of which is that I am a cop and there are certain ideals I should uphold. I will always uphold those ideals and the law so long as I wear the badge and uniform, because it is a trust you the public have given me. These are my personal views and opinions and do not cross over into my vow as a policeman. I even went as far as taking it out completely, then I thought, *Fuck it, let it roll—what're they going to do, arrest me?* God bless the first amendment. I want to say up front that just because I think something should be a certain way for my own personal opinion, satisfaction and glee and that of others doesn't make it right, but only desirable. I will also say that right to some is wrong to others. Potato, potaato. Tomato, tomaato. So much for disclaimers; now that the lawyers have had their say, let's get on with it.

We have had a lot of mass killings by psycho-/sociopaths over the past decade or two, with no end in sight. It seems to be almost a competition now to see who can pull off the worst and most memorable killing. The latest at the time of this writing was an asshole shooting up the LAX airport and killing a TSA officer and wounding others. So what do we do? We catch him alive and take him into custody. That's lawyer talk for now we get to spend millions of our tax dollars on this motherfucker so he can have a fair trial by his peers and then sit in jail the rest of his life or be out on parole in ten years. Explain that to the TSA officer's family so they get it, and while you are at it, make them understand why Daddy isn't coming home again.

A fucker goes into a movie theater and kills twenty-plus people, including children, then stands in the parking lot like he's waiting on a bus till they come and arrest him. Where is he now? In jail waiting on trial, still breathing and in protective custody, so no one in the jail can kill him, and this, gentle readers, is where I have issue. These sacks of shit and all the others like them should have been killed instantly, if not sooner—publicly, brutally, and by the families of the victims and in the same way their loved ones were murdered.

These victims were not given any choice or chance. The closest we have come to doing the right thing recently was with the Boston Marathon bombing by killing one of the brothers and almost the other. But where is the second brother? In jail in protective custody, awaiting his fair trial. In my opinion, they gave up their rights to live and a fair trial the minute they killed others. Did y'all ever stop to think that maybe the reason people murder others so wantonly is because there really is no consequence? What do they care? They go to jail, get three meals a day, TV, exercise, free legal representation, free medical and dental, even an education if they want it. All they have to worry about is keeping their buttholes protected. The tree hugging liberals need to stay the fuck out of it. The Bible says an eye for an eye, Amen.

In this country the government spends about five dollars a day on prisoners and their needs and about one dollar on our students. Inmates have more rights than children and are better protected than children are. What do you think that looks like to the rest of the world?

China has the right idea, as do certain Middle Eastern countries. The punishment fits the crime. You steal; your hand is cut off right away, often without a trial. You hump another man's wife; they drive a spike through your dick. For women they will remove a breast or clitoris. You kill someone; they kill you.

A few years ago I read a great rendition of a trial in China where a guy had killed another guy for money. The trial started about nine in the morning and was over little after ten. They walked him out the back door and put two in his head right there. I love it. The best part is they left him laying there and his family had to come fetch him, pay the government to bury him and had to pay all the court costs and the price of the two bullets. That, my aghast readers, is the shit and the way it should be done in my opinion. Guess what the crime rate is like in China? A lot lower than ours, and they have half the number of people in prison as we do, over 70% of which are on hard labor. This is how they built all the huge projects they have done over there—prison labor. If the prisoners are hurt or die while working for the state, it's up to the family to take care of them; the state don't give a shit

As you have likely figured already, I am all about capital punishment. The same wanton disregard, malice, violence and lack of respect should be inflicted on those who deserve it, swiftly and publicly. Imagine what would happen to the capital crime rate if we started taking these dicks out back and killing them. True to the American way of life, we should also make money at it. If people will pay HBO $7.99 to watch Tom Hanks stranded on a deserted island or comic book heroes save the world for two hours, what do you think they would pay to watch a justified, righteous and sanctioned execution? A bunch, 'cause we as humans are naturally drawn to the violence and the desire of seeing a wrong that is going to be righted. What's one million viewers times $7.99? A truckload of help to someone or something, that's what it is. Take that money and let the people who were wronged decide where it should go, like a victim fund, feed some kids with it, pay off our debts—whatever.

There will always be the malcontents who think it's wrong to take another life for these reasons. I'm not one of those and I don't give a shit about their feelings. I see this as an answer no one wants to engage in for fear of public outcry. Well, how about those that were murdered; don't they get a vote? No one asked them if they wanted to die. Julius Caesar once said, "In order for a leader to do great things for his people, he must think and act in a way that is not always in the best interests of all of the people and pray they see the future rewards in such actions." When you are lying there in the dark one night and can't sleep, ask yourself honestly and truthfully, "What could I really live with, to stop these people from doing what they do to others?" Bet we aren't that far apart.

RESPECT

Respect my friends and daunted readers, is quickly becoming as extinct as T Rex. It is the exception now rather than the rule. The way kids and people under the age of 30 conduct themselves is in my opinion, absolutely out of control. Now I am obviously not including everyone in this, but for the most part youngsters these days are the rudest, most selfish and most self-entitled little shits I have ever met. I heard them referred to once as the "Me generation," and I couldn't agree more.

I guess what bothers me most about all this is their lack of respect and dignity to themselves and by default, to others. President T. Roosevelt once said, "To educate a person in the mind but not in morals is to educate a menace to society." This is true to a fault. These kids have no clue about being proud of something you did or built yourself from the ground up. So why is it like this? Where did our generation fall down in giving them that want and desire? The answer is simple: because we don't allow them to and they don't have to because everything is within reach for them, no effort required. Even the sports stars and music idols these kids look up to don't help one damn bit and often are worse than the kids.

When I was a kid there might be one phone in each of the houses on our road, and about twenty of your neighbors shared it and it was called a party line. You respected others' privacy in that if there was someone on the line, you didn't listen to their conversation. I dare you to find a person not on the phone anywhere you go these days. It seems there is nowhere you can go that you aren't privy to someone's phone conversation or texting. Wouldn't want miss that all important LOL, LMAO, OMG or :). In my opinion, having loud public conversations on your phone or texting others while engaged in conversation with someone is one of the rudest and most disrespectful things you can do. But it is done all the time and no one says a damn thing about it.

Growing up, you did chores and your homework without medicines and without being asked. You listened, did as you were told and did not speak in an adult conversation unless you were spoken to. You would never in a million years consider sassing, cussing or striking your parents. (Siblings were fair game.) You talked to your parents and did things as a family. You may have had a transistor radio and/or a record player if you were lucky. I had my dad's old player and a few "78" records. (Google it if you're staring at the page bewildered; it would take too long to explain without pictures.) We never even had a TV in the house till I was about six and it had three channels you might be able to tune in with a rabbit ear antenna, aluminum foil and holding your mouth just right to bounce the signal off one of the fillings in your teeth.

In school we went to the library and looked shit up with the Dewey decimal system for our school projects and homework that we wrote out by hand that we actually took pride in doing. These days they print it off the Internet and rarely can tell you what it was about. We read books not phones and kindles. I asked a youngster the other day if he knew what a thesaurus was and he had no clue; he thought it was that Greek half man, half horse thing. Remember having to memorize the multiplication tables? In school they taught us long-hand division, multiplication, and Algebra that we did in our head, not with an app on the phone. 'Course, there was no such thing as cell phones then; we had barely invented the transistor radio. Here is an interesting little tidbit for you: the average smart phone today is two hundred times more powerful than the computer that ran the last Apollo mission. That should give you an idea how far we have come and likely why the average current high school graduate has the education equivalent level of a person in grade nine when I went to school. Again, the reason in my humble but educated view is because they are not made to do shit and discipline is in the toilet.

Today there are the Internet, Twitter, Facebook, Instagram, instant messaging, email and texting. With all this up to date technology, we have forgotten the way to communicate in a respectful manner with our fellow man and most of all, our families. We don't have to do it anymore; we can just send a message. It wasn't too long ago I had an entire argument with my daughter by text till I realized what I was doing and called her. You don't see kids playing outside as I did because of Xbox, Playstation, Wii and child predators. Why the fuck should they sit at the table and play a game of cards, checkers or Monopoly when there are zombies and bad guys to be destroyed in the latest game? I will admit, I like playing certain war games on the Xbox but not every day, and I can do the multiplication tables in my head.

When I was a kid one of the things my parents made me do after Christmas was to sit down and write thank you notes to all those who had sent me a present or wishes over the season. We actually sat down and wrote it out, put it in a real envelope with a stamp on it and put it in an actual mailbox. I tried that with my kids once; it did not go well so we settled on emails instead, because the mail box was too far to walk.

So what's my point? What is my rant here? Just this: I believe that the way I was brought up with the values of hard work, honesty and a simpler way of doing things built character in me and most of all, taught me to respect myself and others, plain and simple. These things are being lost to younger generations and I think this is the reason the rates of things like teenage suicide, crime, drug use and pregnancy are the highest they have ever been. They don't know any better. Our society has allowed these kids to be influenced by the easy way out in the world instead of hard work and pride in accomplishing something with their own hands and minds. Because this is lost to them, they have lost respect for themselves and others.

I don't have the magic answer on how to fix this. I wish I did. I'm merely presenting this to you for your thoughts and consideration. If

Douglas McBride

you asked me how I would fix it, I would probably tell you this: Bring them back to a simpler way of things if that's possible and educate them in a way that shows them the value of pride in accomplishment. Set the example and the bar height. Discipline where needed, be consistent in your verbiage and love them, regardless, above all else.

ON BEING A COP

Growing up playing all the games that kids do, cops and robbers was probably my favorite. It was the one I played the most and I was always the cop if I could swing it. Even then and through parts of my adult life, I wanted to be a policeman. It was one of those things that never came to fruition for one reason or another. I did apply one time to a department, passed my entrance exam and was turned down because "I was not physically able". Huh? I passed their PT requirements with no difficulty. What the fuck? Well, as it turned out they were referring to my history of having a broken back. It didn't matter that I had reached and surpassed all the requirements to get in; they basically didn't want damaged goods. Here's the kicker: I applied to this department because I was teaching about 10 of their officers in my martial arts classes. Yeah, I was teaching their officers martial arts but I was not good enough to be one. Really! One thing led to another and time moved on and that idea got shelved but never out of mind really, until I turned fifty.

I don't know what I was thinking except that I had this urge to be a cop again and the opportunity came along to do it. Most people at my age are looking to slow down and do less. Not me, I have to make things more difficult because it's not already that way enough, right? I met this guy and he was a deputy on the reserve department of the local Sheriff's office and told me it's something I should apply to. I did and was accepted, just like that, with no issues or questions on age or spinal issues. I got my uniform and gun and started riding with some of the fulltime guys, and it didn't take me long to figure out that I didn't know shit and everyone else around me knew I didn't know shit. Per my usual approach to not knowing shit, I got books and videos on everything I could find on how to be a policeman and started filling in the vast gaps in my "don't know jack shit" learning curve. I was particularly thankful for John, a full time deputy I rode a lot with, who took me under his wing to teach me what I needed to know. He kept me alive and for the most part, out of trouble and we remain good friends today. Gracias, brother. It took me almost a year to get comfortable and have a good working knowledge about what I was doing out there on the road and the time I spent working at it that eventually paid off.

I also really started to see the differences in a good cop, a bad one and everything in between. Y'all have heard of the term "the thin blue line"? Well, it is supposed to represent the brotherhood, personal and professional connection each cop has for each other and their departments. We stand shoulder to shoulder and do whatever it takes to make sure the other cops working with you go home to their families, including taking a bullet for them. At least that's what it's supposed to stand for, but I have rarely seen it in any consistent form. It may be that way in other departments but the two departments I have worked for couldn't have been further from it. Most cops that are looking to climb the rank ladder are all about covering their ass and what's good for them. I am referring to those who can and will throw any one of us under the bus to make those all important brownie points. The administrator types with knee pads who have the fall guy to take the heat off them when shit goes sideways. These are the ones who don't walk the thin blue line. Let me rephrase this: I have worked with a handful of cops who do walk that line and believe as I do what it stands for, and I am truly honored to have been associated with them. The knee pad gang, uh . . . not so much—truthfully, not at all. In their defense, they are not unique; it's prevalent in all big business and corporate ass-kissing.

Of all the partners I have had, in the situations I have been in on the street, I have never felt unsafe with one of my fellow officers. Being able to say that is a huge deal. We have a saying when something bad has happened and we got through it unscathed. "At least we're going home tonight." To a cop this is what it all boils down to, getting home. When you work with these guys day in and day out, doing some of the shittiest things imaginable, protecting each other and backing each other up, you come to know them and how they will operate in a given scenario. You already know what and how they're going approach it, all without saying a word most of the time. We know we have each other's life in our hands and must do whatever it takes to protect it. If you aren't prepared to do that, other cops you work with are going to know it and won't work with you if at all possible. Cops don't forget and they don't forgive. I know some of you are thinking that this is a little dramatic, maybe, but it is the truth and it is that important.

Ask yourself this question: Who do you call when you hear something outside your window at night, when your neighbor's dog keeps coming to your house to shit in the yard, when there is an accident, fire, shooting, fight, drunk driver, kid missing, someone drowning or hit by a car, an out of control teenager, lock your keys in the car, some crazy motherfucker is loose in your neighborhood, your house has been broken into, someone is driving like an asshole, someone just shot up a junior high or high school, shoplifting, domestic argument, you just saw a drug deal, your kids are using drugs, the cat's drunk, someone drove over the drunk cat and your mail box, something is laying in the middle of the road, your daughter just left with the boyfriend you told her she couldn't see, you think someone you know is going to kill themselves or there is a guy walking around the park with his dick out and some asshole is convinced aliens have landed in his pool. Starting to get the picture? We are called for some of the most bizarre things that are a total waste of time and resources and others that are the most dangerous situations you can think of or imagine. We put our uniforms on every day not just because we get paid to, but because we took an oath "to protect and serve" that most of us actually believe in.

In this country, there is a cop killed every 92 hours and injured every 36 hours in the line of duty. The average cop on the street makes between 11.50 and 18 dollars an hour that are not union. The national average is $13.55. Just to put this in perspective for you, someone working at McDonalds or Burger King makes between $8-$11 starting out, depending on their job description. Recently, the fast food industry workers were protesting and striking to get $15/ hour. Really, for some snot-nosed high school graduate handing out burgers and nuggets, they think $15/hour is fair? Are y'all out of your ever-loving damn minds? They don't carry a gun, don't answer public complaints, get spit on, cussed, hit, shot at or put their life on the line every single time they go to work. I am not well versed on how dangerous a milkshake machine can be but I'm almost positive it won't try to kill you.

To say things have gotten worse for cops over the past 10 years or so, I think, is an understatement. It is a far more dangerous world for us than it was for Joe Friday. These days there is more meth, bath salts, crack, ecstasy, heroin, prostitution, gang wars, automatic weapons and people that think nothing of killing a cop than there was when the Mod Squad was running around. The Simon City Royals, Bloods, Crips, Disciples, Hell's Angels, The Sovereign Citizens and a dozen other gangs and cults are out there vying for drug territories, money, gambling extortion, gun selling, prostitution, murder for hire and ignoring the laws of the land for their own made up laws. This is what we face and fight as cops every day in whatever dose and combination that day brings.

I think to be a cop you have to have and practice a particular mindset. You don't need to be GI Joe or Captain America but you do have to have certain qualities that will keep you safe and alive. First and foremost is you can't lose your mind in bad or intense situations. The "why not" of that statement should be self-evident. You have to have some communication skills to relate to people in all types of circumstances. You have to have patience and a thick skin because people will get in your face. You must be prepared to step it up if the situation warrants it, and you have to be in good physical condition to do this job effectively and safely. Mostly, I think you have to be able to apply common sense and think outside the box independently. I have known cops with these skills and then some, and others who have none. I guess it's that way for all careers but in this one it will get you or someone else killed.

I left my first department after about a year and a half, mainly because it was a huge political arena and I fall very short in this art form, as you might have guessed. A case in point: there was this guy who was just an ordinary patrol cop like me except he was an ass kisser, unlike me, and he was functionally illiterate—no shit, could barely read or write. He and I didn't gee-haw too well because I couldn't trust the bastard not to fuck you over in a New York minute. He had political clout in the department due to family connections and probably some worn out knee pads to show for it. One day I hear this fucker is now the boss. Say what?! How does that work? He totally skipped over corporal, sergeant and lieutenant, straight to being the boss. Wow! Now that's some serious dick sucking. He wasn't even in my give a shit book about all this until he started to mess with me and made life in the department less than tolerable.

I was the only unit available to back up the road sergeant one night in a domestic way out in Podunk country. There is no radio or cell phone reception out here, so I call the shift sergeant, who is also the one answering the call, and clear it to go and back him up. SOP, right? You never let an officer go to a domestic call alone, ever, it's just not done, the reason being is because it has one of the highest percentages of officers getting hurt and killed. It got hairy out there with just the two of us but it was resolved and we got out of there safe. The next day the "Boss" is calling me telling me he's pissed because I went out there without clearing it with him first. This fucker wasn't even on duty and has never made this a requirement before; anyway, he then tells me I disobeyed a direct order not to go out there. Wait a minute, did I come in on a commercial here? Because obviously I have no idea what you are talking about. Well folks, that was enough for me. That incident and a couple of others showed me that they couldn't give a fuck about their officers or their safety so I handed my shit in and left. By this time I had made acquaintances with the deputy chief at the local police department in town because while I was with the previous department, he had asked me to join their SWAT team, which I did. They needed a medic and I needed the experience, so it was a logical step for me to go to that department next. A little background on these two departments might make things a little clearer.

The sheriff's department and the PD were not the best of friends and as you know, it takes two to make an argument. There was always some kind of turmoil between the two departments, and politically it became a real issue at times. For example, the sheriff controlled the jail where we took our prisoners, so the PD was always taking shit for things we didn't do right or for getting into it with the jailers who were being dicks and so on. The joint narcotics task force we had also was run by one of the sheriff's minions. We had officers on it but with little say in it and a source of never-ending bullshit, from what I'm told. Out on the street, the deputies and our officers had no such issues; our jurisdictions often overlapped and we took care of each other because there was no room for egos and politics out there.

The SWAT team was another joint force but was owned and operated by the PD. Because of this the sheriff would slam it every chance he got and publicly stated he did not need a SWAT team and if he did he would get a REAL one from somewhere else. What an asshole. I know what you're thinking; I said joint, right? Well, that's because the only deputy we had on the team was there voluntarily, on his own dime and his own time. We were glad to have him too, 'cause he was a corn-fed country boy, just as stout as they come, and could swing our 60 lb door ram like it was nothing. I have seen this ole boy reach into a car and snatch the driver out of the passenger window with one arm. Each of us on the team had our special skills in one form or another and it was a good mix and we worked hard at making a good team.

I had some great mentors as a rookie cop and these mentors, I am proud to say, are also some of my closest friends. Randy and Jason were my FTOs (Field training officers) at the PD, both good guys, great cops and both combat vet Marines. Both are considerably younger than me (hell, that's about every-damn-body these days), which they made sure I remembered on a daily basis, but they didn't treat me any different and certainly didn't think twice about busting my balls about being a rookie or being an Army grunt. According to these two jarheads there is the Marine corps and then there's everyone else. They put in a lot of time and patience to give me the skills I needed to get my ass to house at the end of shift, and I couldn't have asked for more. Thanks guys, I'm forever in your debt. Oh ya, I nearly forgot, fuck you, Marines! Hooorah!

Randy and I were on the SWAT team together, as well as patrol, so we had some situations come up that got a little hairy. We got a call one night on a guy running around with a gun that was reported as he was going to kill someone and or himself. This asshole was apparently an ex-cop, not too stable and oh yeah, he's in a wheelchair so you'd think it would be easy to spot this guy right? Negative. We looked high and low and could not find the bastard. We finally got him on the phone through his sister and talked him into giving us his location and as it turns out, I had taken care of this guy in the ER before. Randy and I went alone, I approached and Randy was backing me up with the rifle. The short of it was we managed to diffuse a potentially bad situation and we went home.

We were out on a different night looking for this guy wanted on a warrant. We stopped one of the local guys we knew was an associate and conducted what's known as a field interview. He has this woman with him that is drunk and just as mouthy as can be, getting up in our face. She was warned several times to back away but apparently she wasn't listening 'cause the next thing I know she hits me in the chest. Striking an officer is not only a real no-no, but it just plain pisses me off. It's a felony charge so she went to jail, but not before she kicked Randy also. We get her to the jail and the correctional officers are having a time with her. We help and then get out of there. We are called by the chief a few days later saying she is pressing civil charges and we are under investigation. Really? So let me see if I understand this right. This convict has a history of drug and alcohol abuse, a long list of arrests including resisting, drugs, prostitution and a few others. She assaults me and my partner, resists arrest, has drug paraphernalia on her at arrest, she's drunk and fucked up on God knows what, and we are standing in front of the man under Garrity?? This is the only country I know where criminals are innocent until proven guilty, get 3 hots and a cot, free legal defense, paid while in jail, free health care and a gym to work out in every day, but two dedicated cops do their job and we are guilty until proven otherwise. What the fuck, y'all!? That shit is still up in the air at this point, mostly because when a "woman of color" yells civil rights violation it quickly becomes a political issue. In my opinion our chief threw us under the bus and didn't back his officers up like he should have due to potential political fallout. This little scenario just backs up my earlier point about the brass covering their ass.

The rule is once you are commissioned with a department you have two years to go through either the part time or full time Police academy. It just so happens that the academy was not far from where I lived and had an excellent reputation. It was 16 weeks of a very humbling and interesting experience, to say the least. That old expression of "you don't know what you don't know until you've met the teacher" was never a truer word spoken. It was here that I had the privilege of meeting two gentlemen I came to admire both professionally and personally. Captain Fedderico, a high school principal from New Orleans, had the loudest voice attached to kindest personality you ever met. I immediately liked him and respected what he knew and how he taught it to me. This is one of those guys if you saw him on the street you would have no idea he was a cop, let alone the boss over the entire academy and reserve department. The captain is constantly on the move, doing one thing or another, either in the police department or with his school. He is what we down here refer to as a "Coon Ass", which is a Southern term of endearment for someone from Louisiana. Don't ask, because I have no idea what it comes from. The other gentleman is Lieutenant Luke, the original "done it man". Lt Luke was an FBI agent for some 20 + years, he's a lawyer, a Lieutenant in the Sheriff's department and one of the nicest, soft spoken, most intelligent people I know. He is one of those rare people that can size up a problem in a way that will almost always give you a solution. I have had the pleasure of getting to know him and his family, in particular his son who has a lot of dad's qualities. Both of these guys go in the mentor category in my world. Thanks for everything, my friends.

The academy wasn't a walk in the park. It had moments where I would rather have had my scrotum stretched over a rain barrel than to repeat some of the evolutions, the worst probably being the pepper spray. In most departments you have to have been tased in order to be able to carry one and the same rule is applied to the pepper spray. I'm here to tell you, ladies and gents, that shit just frigging hurts. The day of the pepper spray evolution we were told that we would get one stripe sprayed across our face and that would be it. Once sprayed you had to perform certain tasks, and the purpose of this was to simulate that if on the street you deployed your spray and it somehow got in your eyes, you could still function and protect yourself. Well, boys and girls, we had one instructor that day that must have been pissed at something because we got laced all over our faces. It got in my nose, eyes, mouth and even in my frigging ear! You can't just wipe this shit off and get on with your day either because if you wipe, you make it worse. You're supposed to rinse it off with cool water. A good idea in theory but when there was 24 in the class and 2 hoses, you can guess how that went. I will say this, though, the blue line was very evident that day because we took care of each other and made sure everyone made it through. A couple of pointers to pass on for those who might be going the police academy way. Those de-con wipes they sell that's supposed to help with this—don't waste your money. Rinse your face in cool water, sit in front of an air conditioner and ask yourself "Why is it I'm doing this again?"

The Taser is a very effective tool when used correctly. I have had perps who were being mouthy one minute began a whole new tune when the Taser was brought into the picture. As I have stated, to carry one you have to have been hit by one. Well folks, I would take the Taser over pepper spray any day. My biggest concern the day I did my Taser class was whether or not I was going to shit myself, because it has happened. I spent a good part of the day clearing the pipes to somehow ward off that possibility and I'm proud to say I made it home that day with unsoiled drawers and a clearer idea what it means to deploy the Taser. It doesn't really hurt as in pain per se, but it will have your full attention and was the longest 5 second ride I have ever been on, brother. You have to recertify every year on this so you can bet I will be front, center and on time for that class because if you let it expire you have to be tased again. That's a no-brainer, even for me.

Despite what people believe as folklore, cops do not go out of their way to write tickets and pull people over. We also don't eat doughnuts by the box either. The cops I know will pull a car over for one of two reasons: safety or because they want a closer look at you and the inside of the car. Safety can be anything from speeding, to one head light, to a child unrestrained, to shit falling off your car and creating a hazard. Why do we care about that? Because we are the ones that will be filling out the accident and vehicular manslaughter reports till kingdom come if you wreck or cause a wreck that kills someone. Most cops don't want to write tickets 'cause if you want to dispute it, that means a day in court for me and you, and I don't like spending my day off with you. Nothing personal, I just have better things to do is all. This doesn't mean we won't write one. Many a time I have pulled a car over to tell them their lights are out or that was an illegal turn or hey slow it down, trying to be nice doing my job and then letting them go on about their rat killing without a ticket. But, as with everything, there is always the one asshole who just can't seem to help digging themselves a hole to get dropped into. They have to flap their pie hole from the minute I walk up to the car, often before I even had a chance introduce myself or to explain what I stopped them for. I get cussed and treated like shit, so then, my friend, I'm going to write tickets for anything I can find. You will have so many tickets the stack will look like War and Peace when I hand them to you. The last thing I need is to be called into the chief's office to explain a complaint from John Q public on why they just got handed a dissertation in traffic tickets, but I will. If they want to act like an asshole I will be glad to sit there with the chief all day. A word to the wise, oh drivers of the wheeled chariots, the Police don't wake up every day thinking about how we can fuck up your day, so be nice and polite and you will be surprised what you will reap from it.

On the other side of the coin, if we get that warm and fuzzy feeling looking at you or something in the way you drive, act, the type of car or even the number and type of people in the car, you're probably gonna get stopped. To be honest, there is no real science to this; it is a knack or intuition that cops develop to pick out bad guys and bad situations. When I get that "feeling" on someone I pull over, I'm looking real hard for a reason to get in the car because I think this person is not right. By that I mean something about the way they act we call "soft signs" is making me think we have a crime being committed and I look for a reason to search them and the car for drugs, guns, liquor—anything they have hidden. More felony arrests and warrants are picked up by regular patrol cops in traffic stops than any other way and the reason is simple: criminals have to drive to get around so the chances are we are going to get them eventually.

You're in a restaurant and a guy walks in. If he deliberately takes a seat where he can see the rest of the room and the people in it, he's a cop, guaranteed. It drives my wife nuts but it can't be helped; we are just wired that way because of the job we do. Same with walking into a store, movie theater or anywhere public. The first thing I do is get a position in the room where I can see as many of you fuckers as possible. Paranoid, that's what my wife says. Eh . . . maybe so, but I will do whatever I can to protect myself, my family and the public against the bad guys. We are not paranoid so much as we are just hyper-vigilant and prepared. No cop I know goes anywhere without his gun because it is as much a part of us as our underwear and without it we feel more than a little naked.

The last thing I want to say about policeman is on the subject of use of force. We will do what we have to to make it home to the wife, dog and kids. I won't say that there aren't some bad cops out there 'cause there are and they are a fucking disgrace to the badge and profession. These jack-wads deserve everything they get when they are caught because they broke a trust, a trust between you the public and between their fellow officers. What I hate most about bad cops is that because of the few dicks in the crowd, the good cops have the same reputation and nothing could be farther from the truth.

Any given officer walks out the precinct door with his vest, duty weapon, Taser, asp (baton), and possibly pepper spray. In his unit they carry a shotgun and/or a semiautomatic rifle. We are highly trained in all of these weapons and are prepared to deploy them when necessary and needed. Those are the key words here: "when necessary and needed". In the academy, we have it drilled into us about levels of force, deadly force and escalation of circumstances and also when and where each level of force comes into play. Cops are also trained in restraint and reaction, which is the hands-on stuff that cops spend most of their time with as far as force goes—trying to get perps restrained and into handcuffs when they had other plans. Make no mistake about it, if a cop has to draw his weapon something has gone very wrong and you have a major problem if you are on the business end.

Contrary to the way we are portrayed by the press, we don't go out everyday looking for some poor schmuck to shoot, tase or otherwise fuck up with one of our toys every time we get in the car. It's a lot of paperwork and something most of us find very distasteful and don't enjoy doing. Personally, I would much rather you go home or to jail thinking "what a nice policeman" not "that fucking cop tased me and threw me on the ground, what an asshole". To serve and protect, not to whoop ass and fuck shit up.

I am a policeman because of the different opportunities it awards me to help people. I have spent most of my adult life in the service of the public and believe it is a calling that not everyone is capable of or needs to be doing. Is it exciting? Yeah, it sure can be but not like you see it portrayed on TV. Every time one of those actors goes out the door he's shooting somebody or kicking someone's ass. That is nowhere near the reality of being a policeman, nonetheless I could not see myself doing anything else. Being a policeman was once described to me this way: "hours of boredom punctuated by moments of sheer terror." True . . . so very true.

Do me a favor, next time you see a cop, think about what this person does every day to protect you and your family, what little he is paid and the risks they take to do it, and tell them thanks—a small gesture that will so make their day, believe me.

The ER

"Hey doc, EMS is 5 minutes out with a gunshot wound to the chest and they say it's not looking too good," the nurse says. "Dr. Schoop is on the phone wanting to know why we didn't do blood cultures on his patient," the second nurse tells me. "Hey doc, get in here; this guy is crashing!" "The mom in room 14 is pissed and won't leave because you didn't give her any antibiotics for her kid's cold."

This, boys and girls, men and women, is just a small sample of any given moment in my job. For the most part 80% of what we deal with are patients that have nothing at all seriously wrong with them and should not be anywhere near an ER but nonetheless, they still come by the hundreds. It is basically a clinic with some high tech shit in it for the really bad stuff. The ER was described to once sorta the same as it was described to me being a cop: hours of bullshit punctuated by sheer moments of increased pucker tone.

It is for the really sick and seriously messed up folks that we do this job. We take all the high speed training we have had and apply it to saving a life. That in a nutshell is why I do what I do, and for the most part I love my job. I enjoy getting there every day knowing that today will not be the same as yesterday. Some days you're doing clinic the whole shift and others you are ass-deep in blood, guts and bodies all day long. Some ERs are busy; others are not so much. Some have a lot of trauma and bad shit; while others have very little.

The very first time I ever moonlighted in an ER while a resident was a night shift in this little Podunk ER that had 3 rooms in it. What could go wrong, right? Well it did, very wrong. My shift started at 6 pm and by 6:30 I have a mom, eight and a half months pregnant, involved in a car wreck and in big time trouble. Her husband was dead on scene and they took 30 minutes to extricate Mom. They get to me and Mom's belly is split open with blood everywhere and a baby's leg hanging out of it. Mom had an obvious head injury among several other things and was dying right in front of me. Of course the local surgeon is 20-30 minutes away. Let me tell you, at this point my sphincter was so tight you couldn't have pulled a pin out of my ass with a John Deere tractor but I did what I was trained to do. I got the woman paralyzed with some meds and did a c-section right there. She is bleeding like a stuck pig from a tear in her Aorta so I cross-clamped it. Now we are really on the clock because what cross-clamping does is basically cut off arterial supply to the lower part of the body. I got the baby out and went to work on it. He had a fracture to his arm and leg but otherwise seemed ok, but I intubated him just to be safe. I had the respiratory therapy lady, who must have been here the last time Jesus came through, pushing meds and bagging the mom. The lab people were bringing me blood and I had a veterinary assistant who just happened to be there and one RN working with me on the mom. About the time I got Baby taken care of, the surgeon walks in and gets involved with Mom. He fixes the tear and starts putting Humpty Dumpty back together again. We get mom and baby transferred safely to one of the big shops downtown where they both made a full recovery.

This is what ER docs do, all day every day, and it's not like any other discipline in medicine. We have to be pediatrician, obstetrician, neurologist, internal medicine, surgeon, neurosurgeon, and anything else that comes along. We wear a shitload of hats and use them all. Strangely, there is very little thanks in it and we seldom get to know what happens to our patients when they leave the ER, unless we aggressively look into it ourselves. Every once in a while a patient that came in in bad shape or with little hope of seeing another sunrise will pull through and make a point to come and see us to let us know they're grateful and how they are making it. That, my friends, is the shit. That is all we could ever ask for or need in our quest for gratitude. Don't get me wrong; we don't expect to get a pat on the back every time we do our job because it is our job but sometimes on the tough ones, the ones we worried about, it is the best feeling in the world. Me, I worry about very little because I know I did all I could for the patient, win, lose or draw; the rest is in others' hands.

I always said I should write a book about the things that have gone on in the ER but the problem with that kind of book is no one would believe you without pictures. We see some very bizarre shit from all walks of life. If I told you I have one patient that enjoys coming to ER because he likes to stick stuff up his ass, would you believe me? Maybe, sounds legit, right? What if I told you everything he puts up there has to be flesh and blood. Ya, you heard me, flesh and blood like rats, mice, guinea pigs, birds, hamsters—even a lizard one time. Anything that is alive, he crams it up his ass. Still want pictures? How about the lady that's in the ER 2-3 times a week wanting a vaginal exam because her baby won't come out. It's stuck! A mom that brings her 4 week old baby in every day since it was born because she says he is angry with her; that's why he cries. The prostitutes with the multitude of sexually transmitted diseases. The pissed off HIV patients who throw their blood and other body fluids at you. The never-ending line up of drug seekers and their fake medical complaints they act out to get their fix. The 1 year old who has been beat almost to death by his mom because he wouldn't stop crying. The 9 year old who has been caught in a drive-by and now is fighting for his life cause of the bullets in his chest. The 25 year old who has had her abdomen kicked in by her boy friend at 18 weeks pregnant because "he doesn't have time to be a dad right now". I literally have a thousand stories just like these, so I ask again, do you still want pictures? I have learned over the years how to block this shit out when I go home, but it doesn't always work and I have lost plenty of nights' sleep over some but for the most part, I manage. You'd go insane if you didn't.

I really hate some days in this job because we have created a society of pussies and needy motherfuckers who think they are owed everything and have to do nothing for it except show up. We allow them to abuse services because it is "their right". No it's not, because rights are earned where I come from. When I first got into medicine the laws and rules made sense and were about equal for medical providers and the public, but somewhere this got way off track. As it stands right now we as doctors have virtually no rights and all the risk. We are not allowed to tell the noncompliant patient that their diabetes and blood pressure are way out of control because they are not doing what they are supposed to by taking their medicines and being correct in their daily living and diets. Nope, can't fucking say that. I can't tell them that the reason they are in the ER for back pain every damn week is because the spine is not designed to support 300-plus pounds. I can't tell the shocked and surprised mom of the 13 year old that the reason she is about to be a grandmother is that maybe you should have been a little more careful about where she was and who she was with. I can't tell the family of the 19 year old crack addict that just died of a massive heart attack that wishing in hindsight they had done more is redundant and self serving.

I could go on but I'm guessing y'all have the idea. If patients don't like the truth they can complain to the patient advocate and the administration chews our ass most of the time because it affects their numbers and Ganey patient satisfaction scores. It has no bearing whatsoever about what is the truth-hell no, we don't want that. We want the noncompliant asshole that owes the hospital a ton of money he will never pay back to make a complaint so he can continue to abuse the service unmolested. The point is, people are lazy and to compensate they blame others for not taking better care of them instead of them taking care of themselves. Here is one of the best examples of what I'm talking about.

This doc I work with and all the rest of us have dealt with this one crack addict for years who takes his cocaine but not his blood pressure medicine. Every time he comes in his BP is through the roof. We get it down and he leaves after our lecture about stopping his habit and taking his meds. Does he do it? Hell no! This doc sees him one night and does what we always do and sends him on his way. The next day this guy has a stroke and dies. The motherfucker's family then sues the doc for letting him go home knowing he doesn't take his meds and had a cocaine habit. (This, by the way, is another reason I hate lawyers.) Are you kidding me, really? You sacks of shit. Needless to say the case went nowhere but that's not the issue. There is a lot of personal time and anxiety that goes into a lawsuit. It is very taxing mentally, it's embarrassing and it affects the way you practice and your approach to patients.

The issue is these types of people owe thousands of fucking dollars to the hospital and keep coming back and abusing the service. We keep treating them for their bullshit, then they have the nerve and audacity to fucking sue, causing duress and anxiety to a doc who did the right thing. Those kinds of fuckers make me sick, and folks, it's all the damn time, seriously—people will sue over the stupidest bullshit because they think they can bleed a doctor. Ask yourself this, how many businesses do you know where you can go in any time, night and day, demand whatever you want and not have to pay for it, and just walk the fuck out? The answer is none. You can't go to Walmart, load up the cart and walk out with your shit saying, "I'll pay you later". The popo would be on you like stink on shit because in this country we call that stealing. You tell me the difference. Guess I went off on a rant again anyway; I apologize if I have wasted your reading time but not for what I have written. I meant every word.

I have met and worked with some truly amazing people. These are the ones you stand there and go I want to grow up and be just like them. It can be for any reason, nothing special or just something that in your mind is so damn rare it belongs in a museum. My wife says I was born to be a doctor because it seems so easy to me, and it is. In my mind it is a matter of knowing how and what disease is and figuring out which one your patient has and trying to fix it—in a lot of ways, no different than an auto mechanic. Your car makes this funny noise, runs bad or not at all and he figures out what's wrong and fixes it. The only difference is the personal factor 'cause people are afraid of their own mortality. They don't want to be sick and run the risk of dying or being permanently fucked up. That's why we run to the doctor by the thousands every day when we fart in A-minus instead of a B-flat.

As a nation the USA spends more on health care every year than some countries have as a national budget. Millions upon millions of dollars on colds and diarrhea. It was brought to my attention a while back that of the some 3000 plus diseases we know of, we have a cure for about 100 of them. That should give you a great perspective on where we are in the scope of medical practice. We as doctors listen to the funny noise your body is making and hopefully by deduction and a few pointed tests we figure out what's wrong. The big question still remains: can we fix it? It's not like the mechanic who reaches up on the shelf and gets a replacement part; we have to find a way to fix the one that you're already using. We are the guardians of your health, safety, well being and pain.

So what do we get in return for this service? Nothing usually, other than the knowledge and feeling we have done our very best to help you with our limited know-how and resources. Oh yeah, and we get your abuse when you have to wait to be seen, or don't get you what you want, or we don't give you pain meds, or you don't take your meds as we told you and you get sick and decide you need to get a little extra walking around money so you sue. If I had known what path medicine would take this far down the road, I'm not sure I would have gone this way instead of the archaeologist I had considered becoming. Of course, there was always Veterinary school, I guess. Don't get me wrong, I am grateful to have my job and to be able to provide for my family; it's just the bullshit I have to wade through to do it that very much makes me uneasy. Medicine has become the most regulated, over-managed, and most cost in-effective billion dollar business out there, and it's getting worse, not better, with no end in sight. As if it wasn't already a mess, Obama care is really gonna fuck some shit up, you watch.

When I was a kid the town doctor was Dr Wilson. This was a time when house calls were still an integral part of patient care. He would come to the house when he was called, figure out what was wrong with us and root around in his bag for the appropriate medicine for the job, along with the necessary lollipop to make it all better. He would always have a cigarette hanging out of his mouth, smelled of old Spice aftershave and laughed at everything, no matter how dumb it was. As a kid you couldn't be afraid of someone like that, and besides, you were at home and your mom was there—what could go wrong, right? It was a simpler time and medicine, in my opinion, was actually practiced and not performed as it is today.

A few years ago there was a push on by some of the medical community to bring back some of the practices of old and one of these was the house call. Of course this idea was short lived because the fucking insurance companies said they weren't going to pay for it (This is a whole other rant for another time). Personally I don't give a shit; I have been doing house calls for years and consider it a privilege. The people I take care of appreciate it and I feel I have done something for someone who otherwise would have had other problems to deal with on top of health reasons. Case in point: a mom with three kids; one is sick and no car or money. I pride myself on never having charged anyone for this service . . . well, there was that time a neighbor down the street came and got me in the middle of the night and I had the pleasure of delivering his son on the kitchen floor. He showed up at my house a week later with two chickens as payment he felt I was due. I politely refused and gave them back, so instead, he named the boy after me and that, my fellow planet dwellers, is truly an honor I wear most proudly.

The strange part of all this is I did not start out in ER medicine. I originally considered it but changed my mind and did a residency in Pediatrics. I practiced in an office a number of years and gradually made my way into ER medicine and eventually became medically boarded in both. It's kind of a weird combination, pediatrics and adult ER, but WTF, I'm all about going a different path just for the shits and giggles. I still wake every morning on work days with a desire to save those I can and educate those who are the future of medicine. For several years I have held an Associate Professor position in two major medical schools. I have discovered that this is a very rewarding and fun way to practice medicine. Not only that, it forces me to be a better doctor and stay on top of my game. These kids are energetic, intelligent and curious, so the old man always has to be that little bit ahead. They challenge me and I accept that for what it is, the same way Obeone and others did in my day. Maybe one day my feet will be big enough to wear their shoes. We'll just have to wait and see, I guess.

KATRINA

Now here was a good time, readers. Three whole weeks of sunshine with 98% humidity and scattered rain storms that would make Noah start another project and plentiful disease with no power, fuel, transportation, clean water or sanitation, coupled with civil unrest, murder, looting, neglect, and abandonment. Welcome to the Mississippi coast, ladies and gents; pull up a rock and sit down. I've got a story I'm fixin' to tell y'all.

My fellow adventurers, I shit thee not on three weeks either; technically it was more like six weeks before things hit some semblance of normal. I know at my house we were well into the fourth week before we had all the amenities back. For those of you who don't know, Katrina was a category five hurricane, a 250 mile wide force of natural destruction that covered the coast and inland from Louisiana to Alabama to as far north as Arkansas. The problem with her was she moved so slow that she just kept pounding you for hours on end. Anything in her way was devastated, destroyed and made to disappear like it was never there.

I say my house 'cause it was the only one I had left that was still livable as long as it didn't rain, which was bound to happen on a daily basis. I had just purchased a brick rental house about two hundred yards from the beach three weeks before this bitch blew into town; now I can't find the house or any of the shit that was in it. Gone, vanished, just a slab where it used to be. I went down there to check on it two days after the storm and the only way I even knew where it might be was by landmarks that had survived. I was nowhere near alone on this, as you have already smartly surmised; just about every house down there within a half mile of the beach was MIA. Most were stacked in a not so neat pile 4 stories high against the railway embankment and smashed to shit. The day before the storm I did all I could to make sure the house was not too damaged. I even boarded up the windows. Yeah, that helped tremendously, didn't it?

At the time I was the medical director and the chief of staff of a small hospital about 20 miles north of the coast. This distance did not give us any slack from the storm and this was where my other house was, with the shitty roof. For four days and nights I was in that hospital with no one else but the staff and me to tend to folks, and mama, tend we did. The hospital fared pretty well through the storm; there was damage but not on the scale it could have been, and it was useable in the parts that mattered. As I said, I was the only doc so I was busy, like a one-legged man in an ass kicking contest kinda busy. The hospital had a generator so we had some amenities and there was food but what really got to be a pain is that people were leaving the coast heading to us in droves, thinking the grass was still green here. They couldn't have been more wrong because we had just as many issues as, if not more issues than, they did. The government wasn't getting off their ass to help anyone, so they weren't worth a shit and in fact they didn't even bother to show up till 3 days later. Hell, there were people from New York, Minnesota, California and the rest of the damn country that had gotten there faster and were more help than our government. Shit, don't get me started on another rant.

People started showing up at the hospital wanting shelter and food, and we just didn't have it. It got to the point where I had to call in the National Guard to protect us because people were trying to break in and steal shit. The guard showed up with two Humvees with 50 caliber machine guns on them and that got the message out loud and clear. We turned no one away medically, but we barely had what we needed to take care of our patients and the staff that now temporarily resided at the hospital. To make matters worse, our referral hospital that takes all the patients we do not have services for, like critical care, for example, was closed because it was under water, and they were another 25 miles north of us. What that meant to was we kept these patients, got our hearts and minds right and did our best. The nursing and support staff had to do some serious learning in a big hurry but they stepped up and got the job done and I was very proud of each of them.

I had been in disasters before, just never on this scale, and what I took home from Katrina was this. There are those that when things get rough will step up, do what needs to done and in doing so will make sure the person to their right and left is also squared away. These awesome people unfortunately make up the minority. The majority are the motherfuckers that take care of only themselves and couldn't give shit about anyone else, including their own kin. And buddy, when shit hit the fan you found out quick fast and in a hurry just which one was which. I have been ashamed of the human race at different times for things we have done to ourselves, each other and this planet and this little fiasco was right up there in the top five. Some people even let others die to save themselves—who does this? In the military it is pounded into you about taking care of the man next to you and not abandoning your post. Some people instinctively know this and it is already a part of their character, while others couldn't find it if it was handed to them wrapped in a bow.

The epilog of this story is that I had to medically do some things that were outside the box, only because I had nowhere else to turn. They brought a seizing 14 year old to me one night who earlier in the day had a tree fall on his head helping his dad clear some roads. Basically he had a bleed in his head and I had nowhere to send him and had to do something or he was going to die. I got a battery operated drill out of my truck, took my best guess and drilled a hole in the kid's skull. Apparently I got it right because I saw him walking around Walmart about eight months later. Would I do it again? You betcha, because that's what needed to be done. There are a million stories of people who went above and beyond doing what was needed to be done in Katrina, and because they did, made it just a little easier on everyone else. Well done, my friends, well done—you are all heroes in my book.

I won't tell you that in the subsequent years, every time the weather dude got on the box and said there was a hurricane headed our way that I didn't tighten the ole sphincter just a tad because I'd be lying. I don't want to do that again—ever. If I had to well, ok, let'er rip, I will face whatever I have to and do it with the same honor, courage and integrity shown me by others. I learned from the last one, so I will be a little better prepared the next go-around. These things are sent to try us via our hearts, minds and souls, but it's always about how we rise to meet them that defines us as beings, the predator or prey, the strong or the weak. The best thing is, you get to decide which you want to be.

On Fighting Age

Triathlons are a blast! Doing the training isn't but racing, hell yeah, it's about the most fun you can have with your clothes on. I fell into racing because I was starting to get fat. I lived up in north Alabama and seemed to be working all the time, wasn't doing martial arts or any other kind of exercise and pretty much eating whatever I felt like. I'm like forty years old and Ronni had just got here, the ex-wife had just took off to Mississippi with a divorce and kid so I developed a "whatever the fuck" kinda shitty attitude that wore on my health. I was around the 220 mark which is about 30 lbs over where I should have been, so I started going to the local gym. You ever tried to carry 30 extra pounds on a treadmill? It ain't easy or fun, I'm just saying.

Anyway, I'm well on my way to a heart attack on the treadmill one day and I see this Triathlon on the TV. It looked like fun and a good way to get back into shape and I already knew how to run and ride a bike (so I thought). The swimming would take a little work but it was doable (so I thought). The facts are these, boys and girls, though I know how to do these events individually, however poorly, doing them in succession and at set distances and under race conditions was a whole other animal. Of course, me being the smart ass that I am, I want to get started on this, thinking it's not going to be a problem so I jump off the treadmill with my extra 30 pounds and into the pool. It was only 25 yards one way and folks, I didn't think I was going to make it Holy shit, did I have some work to do. I am one of those people who doesn't see the mountain, just the problem of how I'm going to climb it. I do not like being beat at anything; I don't care about losing, I just won't lay down and let something beat me cause now it's a matter of pride and being as stubborn as a Missouri mule, I suppose.

Triathlons are a Swim, Bike and Run in that order and they do it that way for a reason, because you don't want to be doing the swim after you have run 26 miles and biked 112—trust me on this one. It's hard enough to do it the right way around without having to worry about drowning. There are basically three categories of tri's and they are based on distance. Sprint is the smallest and is usually a 200-600 yd swim, 8-15 mile bike, 2-3 mile run. This is how I got started and I thought that toward the end of the race I was going to die. Oh my God! I was dragging ass and sucking wind across that finish line. It was about here I realized I had better step up the training a little more than just the few weeks I put in and get in a little better shape to do this again.

The next several months were heavy duty hardship on the body but gradually I got better. Try riding a bike as hard as you can for 5 miles then jump off and run 1 mile, then you will get an idea how difficult this shit can be. I got very obsessed with training and racing, to the point it governed my life for a while. I can't tell you why, other than I was in the best shape of my life, I was down to 160 lbs and there was nothing like the high of crossing that finish line.

Tri-athletes are a very odd bunch and one of our obsessions is always trying to race faster. Every time we toe the line we are trying to beat ourselves again. This is the only sport I know that the common man can race side by side with the pros. Tri-athletes come from all walks of life, all ages, size, shape, and description, so there are no egos in this sport, which is a nice change. I have seen it over and over again, athletes taking care of each other out on the course because it is not a competition with others so much as a personal battle with yourself to get better.

As an example, I was on the bike leg of a race and this big girl blew by me like I was standing still. I pride myself on the bike being my strong suit but this girl left me in the dirt. I did my best to catch her for 20 miles but at the end of bike leg she was nowhere to be seen. I finally caught her 3 miles into the run and she, I came to find out, was a very nice lady and I admired her determination and athleticism. Like I said, all types and you never underestimated anyone.

I was always looking for the next great challenge so it was a natural progression to one day do an Ironman race. This is the holy grail of the triathlons, the big kahuna that is 2.4 mile swim, 112 mile bike and 26.2 mile run for a grand total of 140 miles of hell, all in one day. The pros do these races in under 8 hours, which to me is just the 8th wonder of the world. You have to be some kinda athlete to just do one of these events to any degree of good, but all of them! To put this in perspective, these pros are running the marathon at the end in under 3 hours, some under 2.5 hours. That's enough to qualify for the Boston marathon and be ranked in the top pro runners. This is after the bike ride where they average 25-30 MPH which is around the average speed of the Peloton in the Tour De France. Get the picture?

To train for one of these races you picked the race or races a year out. I spent about 20-30 hours a week training, and I am not proud to say that this was often at the cost of time with my family, but there is a lot that goes into it: nutrition, recovery, weight training, equipment maintenance, etc. No excuse, I know, but that's all I got, as weak as it is. I did several Ironman races over about 3 years and got to travel to race in places like Western Australia, Arizona, London and others.

One of the best races I ever did was called "Escape from Alcatraz" in San Francisco. Ya, that Alcatraz. They take you out to Alcatraz Island on this ferry at 6 am and kick you off. Now folks, the old saying about San Francisco: "The coldest winter I ever spent was the summer in San Francisco" is no bullshit. Mid-frigging July and the temp is in the 60s and the water was a balmy 48 degrees that morning! It was a 1.5 mile swim and very difficult because of the current, so if Frank Morris and the boys survived their escape in 1962, my hat's off to you, gentleman, you earned that freedom the hard way for sure. I had no problem with the swim, really; it was the bike that kicked my ass because it was 18 miles up and down this big-ass steep hill, to and from the presidio. Of course, me being from the Southern coast didn't help with training for hills 'cause we don't have any. The run was 8 miles along the beach and absolutely beautiful. The day before the race, just so I could say I did, I went for a bike ride across the Golden Gate Bridge to Sausalito and back, and it was absolutely spectacular. I guess I trained and raced

Ironmans non-stop for about 3 years until one day at a race it caught up to my body and I really thought I was dying.

I had noticed in the weeks before the race I was feeling tired a lot and was not up to snuff as far as training went but I ignored this, as it can happen with athletes from time to time. The first rule in any athletics is listen to your body, and I didn't listen. I was doing this small race in Louisiana as a training race for an upcoming Iron Man and as soon as I got in the water I knew something was wrong because I had nothing. It took me an hour to swim a mile and once out of the water I was just exhausted, but I pressed on and started the bike leg. Stubborn AND stupid, I guess, 'cause what I should have done is shut it down right then. At twenty miles into the twenty-five I was getting nauseated, my head was pounding; I was dizzy and plain felt fucking horrible.

I was dead last into the transition area and I have never been dead last ever; I'm usually somewhere in the middle of the pack. I got to transition, bent down to put my running shoes on and fell over on my face and couldn't stand. I was disoriented and sick to stomach, my heart was pounding and I felt like someone had pulled my drain plug and all my insides were pouring out of me somewhere. I was lying there heading for unconsciousness and could do nothing about it. This ain't good, boys and girls. My wife and little girl were there and they knew something was wrong because I kept trying to get up and couldn't. Everything went fuzzy and then it was black hole time for a few minutes. I wasn't really out but I wasn't here, either. I could hear my wife and daughter but couldn't understand them or focus on them, and I started to think I was having a stroke or worse. I guess I lay there a bit and things got a little more normal till finally I was able to collect all my toys and left the sandbox.

I stayed screwed up for about 3 months 'cause I reckon I just pushed my body past what it was able to compensate for anymore. Hindsight being the great teacher that it is, I figured out that I had been training and racing non-stop almost 3 years and finally my body just said "Fuck you, asshole, I need a vacation." The epilog to this was I did not race again until the next year 'cause I just didn't have the juice to do it. I only raced twice in that year and as of this writing I have not raced in 2 years. I sure do miss it, though, and I actually got my bike out this year and rode some. I'm really starting to think I will try to race again next year. What I'd really like to do is the 500 mile non-stop endurance race through Death Valley—that sounds like the perfect way to mess up my shit once again.

I started lifting weights a lot in the past few years and packed on some weight. I raced at around 155 lbs, I'm now around 200 lbs and strong as hell. Last summer I got up to 215 but even though I'm carrying muscle as opposed to fat, I didn't feel good that heavy, even though size has its privileges at that weight. I got back to running and lost ten or so lbs and felt much better. I like to lift several times a week because it is a never-ending challenge of "Let's see what I can do today" kinda mentality. Most people think it's just a bunch of steroid-taking Neanderthals that lift weights all the time and that couldn't be further from the truth. Even the Pope lifts weights—ya, that Pope. It takes more concentration than you think, not like advanced calculus kinda concentration but concentration nonetheless.

Ultimately I would like to seek a balance of racing and lifting as the way to stay in shape and healthy. It has become very apparent to me in the past few years that I have creaks and groans that match the wrinkles on my ass as a sure sign I am on the back nine, not the front, so I have made it my quest to fight it every step of the way. I look around at some guys half my age and know I am way ahead of them in condition of mind and body because I work at it and they don't, plus I want to get some decent mileage out of this body. My rule is, "It is easier to maintain than it is to catch up." I know one day it will come to an end but I will have the satisfaction of saying it wasn't from anything I didn't do. Studies have shown that being healthy and exercising regularly statistically do not allow you to live any longer than those who do not; you're just healthier and live better, I think. I say cram the stats up your ass and let's see what happens.

THE LAST VERSE

So wada'ya think? Not too bad for a redneck who can't even spell, I suppose. I think I have finally run out of bullshit to tell you and that, my wife will tell you, is no small feat in itself. In a way, I am a little saddened to think I'm done because it has been a blast doing this. I have probably said too much in some places and not enough in others, and I suppose there were things I wanted to put in but felt were way too personal and others I should have thought that way on and left out. Oh well, who gives a shit, right? I already confessed to not knowing what I was doing when I started this little shindig.

As far as I know I have told the truth other than some legal name change shit to stop someone from getting pissed off and trying to sue me. As for the rest, well . . . there maybe a little embellishment here and there. Like I said at the beginning, if you think I'm talking about you, prove it. The First Amendment still stands, regardless of how fucked up the government seems to be getting. To be honest, I think the Founding Fathers would be ashamed of us; I know there are times when I am. Even though I took an oath to stand and defend this country, I don't always agree with our politics.

This started out as an experiment that turned in to a project and from there became an act of love, obsession and catharsis. Mostly, I learned a lot about myself and the nudges on the road to this point that I hated, loved, tried to forget, did wrong, did right and wished I could do again. In my simple mind, we are basically all jigsaw puzzles that are put together with the experiences we've had and the people we shared them with. I would change nothing, not a thing—even the parts that hurt more than I thought I could ever bear but found out I could. As Tecumseh said, "When it comes your time to die, be not like those whose hearts are filled with the fear of death, so the when their time comes they weep and pray for a little more time to live their lives over again in a different way. Sing your death song and die like a hero going home." I truly believe this because I have never been afraid of dying, just how I went and if given a choice, I would like to go quickly. I don't care how, just quick and preferably with a smile on my face.

Other than some aches and pains that come with old age and trashed knees from the abuse inflicted on this body over several decades, I can still get around like someone half my age and I plan to get my money's worth out of this carcass before I turn it in. I have always sort of looked up to, tried to include and emulate famous people who in some way inspired me along the way: Martin Luther King, JFK, T. Roosevelt, Winston Churchill, Abraham Lincoln and General George Patton to name a few. These people and others like them have in some way shaped changed and left their impression on the world because of who they were and their actions. I don't want to end up in a history book but I want people to remember me for something I did to or for them that in some small way was important in their lives. To my way of thinking, there is no greater epitaph. The people I really look up to are the people in my life on an almost daily basis: my friends, family, coworkers and you, the people I take care of and interact with on a daily basis, because without you, life would pretty much be like watching grass grow. Y'all are the spice of my day to day existence, and I appreciate each of you.

I don't have the "bucket list" that seems to be the favorite catch phrase currently. I have some things that I want to do before I leave this peculiar little mess called Earth, and there are places and wonders I want to cross off my "Yup, been there-seen that shit" list. If I could ever get rid of my kids, I might stand a prayer at doing it. Naaaahh, I love the little shits. I'd take nothing for 'em and I would just miss them more than I already do when I don't see them for a while.

I want to jump out of an airplane at fifteen thousand feet 'cause that sounds like a rush I wouldn't forgive myself for missing. Back in the 80s I actually went to ground school for skydiving but I broke my ankle at one of the practices and as life usually goes, it got put on the back burner and never finished. I want to have my picture taken in front of each of the wonders of the world. I want to make a difference in someone's life because of something I did to help them and never know about it. I want to grow old in peace, with no regrets. I would like to take an air balloon across the country. I want to save a soldier who has been hurt on the battlefield and get him back to his family. I want to go on a quest for the most beautiful sunset in the world. I would like to have a conversation with the Dalai Lama. I want racism to be something you read about in history books. I would like to go ghost hunting and catch one of the little bastards. (I know, strange right? Can't help it, it's the way my mind works.) I would like to ride my bicycle across Europe. Finally, I want to see the world finally and truly at peace.

In reading this manuscript over during the editing phase, I was reminded of a quote that was given at President John F. Kennedy's funeral by his brother Robert: "Some men see things as they are and ask why, I dream of things that never were and say why not." I believe that is also me, folks, always looking for something other than what's in front of me. The glass is always half full in my world. I could go on and on but you have had enough of me for a while, and it's time to go.

This is the part where I get to thank a bunch of people for all their help; God knows how I'm gonna get that done. Y'all know who you are and how truly grateful I am. Most of all I want to thank you the readers for taking the time to peek into my funny little world; it has been an honor and a pleasure. It is my hope that I have entertained you in some small way and maybe gave you pause for thought in others. Hopefully, I was able to steer some of you away from making similar mistakes that I have made and convinced you that anything is possible if you want it badly enough. To those who took the time out of their own busy lives to proof this for me and let me know it wasn't a piece of shit, to my wife and kids for their encouragement and to my fellow boys in blue for making sure I got home to finish it, thank you just doesn't seem to cut it somehow, and I fall short on the words to express my feelings.

As I said from the beginning, I am an ordinary man, the product of a not-so-ordinary world, but aren't we all? To my family, who have raised me as much as I have them, I love you all from the very deepest of places within, and with a passion I could never explain. I wish my family, friends and you the reader a long life, with all the love, adventure and excitement you can stand and then some.

See Ya.